Malcolm Dillon

The History and Development of Banking in Ireland

From the earliest times to the present day

Malcolm Dillon

The History and Development of Banking in Ireland
From the earliest times to the present day

ISBN/EAN: 9783337322816

Printed in Europe, USA, Canada, Australia, Japan

Cover: Foto ©ninafisch / pixelio.de

More available books at **www.hansebooks.com**

THE HISTORY AND DEVELOPMENT OF BANKING IN IRELAND FROM THE EARLIEST TIMES TO THE PRESENT DAY.

BY

MALCOLM DILLON.

London:

EFFINGHAM WILSON & Co., ROYAL EXCHANGE.

BLADES, EAST & BLADES, 23, ABCHURCH LANE, E.C.

Dublin:

ALEX. THOM & CO., LIMITED, 87, 88, & 89, MIDDLE ABBEY STREET.

1889.

PREFACE.

The Author had the honour to read in December, 1885, before the Institute of Bankers in London, a paper on "Banks and Bankers in Ireland"—a subject which had, hitherto, received but scant attention from historians. The interest attaching to matters affecting Ireland at the present time, the absence of any work dealing exclusively with banking in the Sister Kingdom, and the circumstance that the *Journal* of the Institute in which the paper is recorded is now out of print, has suggested its reproduction in this greatly extended form, with the events brought down to the present date.

LONDON, *June*, 1889.

CONTENTS.

FRONTISPIECE.

Fac-simile of Bank of Ireland One Pound Note, dated March 4, 1808.

CHAPTER I.

INTRODUCTORY.

CHAPTER II.

IRISH COINAGE AND CURRENCY.

CHAPTER III.

EARLY HISTORY OF IRISH BANKING. THE PRIVATE BANKS.

CHAPTER IV.

PRIVATE BANKS—*continued.*

CHAPTER V.

THE BANK OF IRELAND.

CHAPTER VI.

THE PROVINCIAL BANK OF IRELAND.

CHAPTER VII.

The Irish Joint Stock Banks.

CHAPTER VIII.

Failed Banks.—The Agricultural and Commercial Bank of Ireland and the Southern Bank of Ireland.

CHAPTER IX.

The Tipperary Joint Stock Bank.

CHAPTER X.

Unsuccessful Banks.—The London and Dublin Bank, the Union Bank of Ireland, the English and Irish, the European, and the Munster Banks.

CHAPTER XI.

The Irish Banking Act.

CHAPTER XII.

Savings Banks and Loan Funds.

PAGE

Origin of Trustee Savings Banks—Extension of the system to Ireland—Legislation—Rates of interest allowed—Losses by fraud—Investigation as to the failure of the Tralee Bank—Offer of the National Bank in 1848 to receive deposits of ten shillings—Institution of Post Office Savings Banks—Private hoarding—Statistics—Runs on Savings banks—Pawnbrokers in Ireland—Monts de Piété—Practice of pawning Bank notes and money—Charitable Loan Funds—Origin—Rates of interest charged—Progress of the Loan Funds—Comparative operation 1838–1888.... 103

CHAPTER XIII.

Statistics.

Progress compared with England and Scotland—Population—Deposits, and average deposits per head 1840–1888—Remarks on the Table—Movements of banking capital, 1846–1888—Bank note circulation, 1844–1888—Average circulation, per head of population, in selected years. ... 110

APPENDIX.

THE HISTORY AND DEVELOPMENT OF BANKING IN IRELAND.

CHAPTER I.

INTRODUCTORY.

Analogy between the banking systems of England and Ireland—Obstacles which checked the development of Irish banking—Political agitation—Home Rule—Agitation directed against individual banks—Burning of Alderman Beresford's notes—Ignorance and simplicity of the people—Popular notions of banking—Liability of the Irish to panic—Run on the Savings banks—The potato famine—Decreasing population—Absenteeism—The Encumbered Estates Court—Bank of Ireland monopoly—Banks which have failed or discontinued business—Existing joint stock banks—Liability of shareholders.

THE main features of banking in Ireland are, in many respects, a reproduction of banking experiences in England. A parent bank, connected with the State, established under a charter almost identical in terms with that granted to the Bank of England, enjoyed until comparatively recent years, the like privileges. The same uncontrolled system of private banking which marked the early history of banking in England also existed in Ireland, and was attended by similarly unhappy results. Lastly, the gradual removal of restrictions on banking enterprise rendered possible the establishment of joint stock banks, adapted to the wants of the people, and extending and developing in the same remarkable manner, the trade and resources of the country. But, here, the points of resemblance may be said to cease, as Ireland is an agricultural rather than a commercial country.

The development of banking in Ireland has, however, been checked by obstacles which are either peculiar to that country, or, if they exist elsewhere, are less marked and not so far-reaching in their effects. Foremost among these may be placed the *Political Agitation* to which the country has been subject, to a greater or less extent, during the whole period embraced in the review of banking. Whether the end to be secured be legitimate or not, it cannot be doubted that the effect of agitation is to create a feeling of insecurity, and thus to embarrass trade, and to destroy confidence. Moreover, to destroy confidence is not only to stop the inflow of capital, but also to encourage its withdrawal,—a tendency which has, of late, been more than usually marked—to the obvious prejudice of banking progress. A noteworthy instance of the disturbing effect of political insecurity was afforded in December, 1885, when, immediately following Mr. Gladstone's supposed declaration in favour of Home Rule, the Stock of the Bank of Ireland, which stood at the commencement of the year at £336, fell from £300 on December 17th, to £249 on December 28th. It was sought to show at the time that the fall in the price of the Stock was due to the decreased dividend just then announced, but the relative effect of the two causes is evident from the fact that a precisely similar fall in 1879 caused a decline of only £8 10*s*. per share.*

---

* The following are the highest and lowest prices of Bank of Ireland stock during the years named :—

Year.	Highest.	Lowest.	Year.	Highest.	Lowest.	Year.	Highest.	Lowest.
	£	£		£	£		£	£
1875	308	297½	1880	311½	299¾	1885	338	249
1876	312	300	1881	318¾	307¾	1886	285	250
1877	315	307	1882	327	311	1887	291	273
1878	316¼	307⅞	1883	331	316	1888	310	280
1879	313	295½	1884	340½	325¼	—	—	—

Sometimes the agitation has been directed against the banks individually. Such an instance occurred in August, 1885, when "United Ireland," one of the organs of the Nationalist party, published in Dublin, charged the Bank of Ireland with "strangling" the Munster Bank, adding that if the mischief were not undone, "Irish public opinion would demand the stripping of the bank of its indefensible and ill-used monopoly of public money." It will be unnecessary to enter into the details of this almost baseless charge, further than to state that the Munster Bank having, on the eve of suspension, applied to the Bank of Ireland for assistance, declined the terms on which the assistance was offered. About the same time some articles in a similar tone appeared in the "Freeman's Journal," another Nationalist organ, with the result that a run commenced in September on the Munster branches of the Bank of Ireland, which put the bank to the expense of importing a million sterling in gold from England, to meet it. In consequence of this also, the Stock which stood at £327 on September 1st, fell by December 1st to £306.

Thus, viewed from a purely banking standpoint, the efforts of Irish patriots have not been in the direction of encouraging commercial enterprise. The instances recorded above are of quite recent date, but the same feeling has always existed. It found expression in a curious manner in the year 1798, when Alderman and Lord Mayor Beresford, a Dublin banker, who had been very active in instituting proceedings against the rebels, and who had in this way made himself obnoxious to a section of the populace, was regaled with the sight of a public bonfire of his own notes, the crowd dancing round it, and crying out, while the "promises to pay" were being reduced to ashes, "What will he do now? His bank will surely break."

Again, *the ignorance and simplicity of the people* has been a difficulty to surmount. The growth of banking in all countries has been slow, and popular notions on the subject have not always kept pace with the progress made. But nowhere has the want of acquaintance with banking principles and practice been so marked as in Ireland. Nor has it been confined to the peasantry and lower orders. Even among the mercantile community, and within quite recent years, the functions of banking were hardly understood.

The Bank of England was founded in 1694, and the Bank of Scotland in the following year, but the Bank of Ireland was not established until nearly a century later. For a long period, therefore, the credit organisation of the country was in the hands of a number of so-called bankers, individuals with little or no capital, but issuing notes without restriction, who were enabled to trade on the credulity of the people. The Joint Stock Banks had to combat with the revulsion of feeling against banking, which was occasioned by the general and disastrous collapse of these private note-mongers.

The *liability of the people to panic* must have been a standing menace to banking prosperity. Any cause, whether social or political, the failure of banks at home or at a distance, was sufficient to create a run for gold. Even the Savings banks were not free from this liability. In 1846, there was a run upon the Savings banks in the South of Ireland which originated in the fear of depositors that it should be known they had so much money at command, and that the knowledge should operate against them in their endeavours to evade or beat down the demands of their landlords. An instance of a run arising out of circumstances of political excitement is recorded on a preceding page. In other countries, panics when they have taken place, have been due to reasonable and generally sufficient causes, but in Ireland the flimsiest pretext seemed enough to create a run on the banks, involving them in the cost and risk attending the movement of gold. The progress of education, and the stability of the Joint Stock Banks, has done much to remove this tendency, though, however, in a mitigated form, it still exists.

The great *Potato Famine* of 1846–1847 which reduced the country to a condition of almost utter desolation, was a further hindrance to banking progress, and the distress it occasioned was felt during many succeeding years. It is estimated that during a similar famine in 1739, one-fifth of the whole population perished, and between 1831 and 1842, six seasons of dearth were experienced of a more or less partial character.

In this connection the influence on banking of a *decreasing population*, should be mentioned. At the beginning of the century the population was about 6,000,000, and it increased progressively until the highest point was touched, viz. :—8,295,061 in 1845, the year just preceding the potato famine. Since that date, with an unimportant exception in 1877, there has been a steady decline. In 1851 the population fell to 6,552,385, in 1861 to 5,798,967, in 1871 to 5,412,377, in 1881 to 5,174,836, and in 1888 to 4,777,545. This decline, due in the first instance to the loss of life consequent on the failure of the potato crop is also, in part, attributable to emigration.

Absenteeism has been another impediment to the progress of banking in Ireland, and in the early history of the country it must have constituted a real grievance. Sir William Petty, writing in 1672, estimated that one-fourth of the real and personal property was held by absentees. Prior, in a list published in 1729,* divides them into three classes—those who were seldom or never seen in Ireland, those who visited the country for a month or two, and those who were occasionally absent. He estimated the amount of money derived from, but spent out of, the country by the first class at £204,200, by the second at £91,800, and by the third at £54,000, making, with the amounts drawn by pensioners, &c., an annual sum of £627,799 3*s.* 1*d.* Another account, published in 1769, places the total income spent out of the country at £1,508,982 14*s.* 6*d.*† Arthur Young gives the rental of absentees, about the same period, as £732,200, equal to one-seventh of the whole estimated rental; and, according to Swift, one-third of the rental of Ireland was spent in England. Absenteeism continued to increase until the close of the French war, in 1816, and, although it diminished from that time, a substitute for many of its evils was supplied by the rapid impoverishment of a large number of idle and extravagant squireens.‡ To help in freeing the country from this incubus an Act was passed in 1848 to facilitate the sale of incumbered estates, which, however, proved wholly ineffectual, and was superseded by another in the following year, appointing a commission of three persons to constitute a Court for the purpose. This Court was reconstituted in 1859, on a permanent footing, under the

---

* List of lords, gentlemen, and others who having estates, employment, and pensions in Ireland spend the same abroad.

† A list of the absentees of Ireland. Dublin, 1769.

‡ Encyclopædia Britannica, Vol. XIII., 1881.

title of the Landed Estates Court, after having effected 3,547 sales, amounting to £25,190,839. The result of the operations of the Encumbered Estates Court has been to increase the number of estates of medium size, and probably to lessen the number of absentees. It appears from a return presented to the House of Commons in 1872, that, in 1870, about 25 per cent. of the soil was owned by absentee proprietors and about 26 per cent. by proprietors who, though living in Ireland, were not resident on their properties.

Lastly, the obstruction to banking progress caused by the *Bank of Ireland monopoly* must be briefly touched upon. This subject is entered into more fully in succeeding chapters, and it is only necessary to state here that the bank enjoyed what was practically an entire monopoly of the banking business of the country from 1782 to 1825, and a partial monopoly from 1825 to 1845 when the remainder of its exclusive privileges were swept away. These privileges delayed, until 1825, the establishment of joint stock banks, and the inflow of English capital, while the deficient banking accommodation retarded trade and caused considerable distress.

Since the passing of the Act of 1825, four banks have failed. They are :—

	Established.	Failed.
The Agricultural Bank of Ireland	1834	1841.
The Southern Bank of Ireland	1837	1837.
The Tipperary Joint Stock Bank	1838	1856.
The Munster Bank	1864	1885.

The following banks retired from business :—

	Established.	Retired.	Business transferred to—
London and Dublin Bank ...	1843	1848	National Bank.
Union Bank of Ireland ...	1862	1868	Munster Bank. Hibernian Bank.
English and Irish Bank ...	1863	1864	European Bank.
European Bank, Dublin Branch	1864	1865	Munster Bank.

The following is a list of the existing banks in the order of their establishment, with their capitals, reserves, and authorised issues :—

Name of Bank.	Established.	Capital.		Reserve Fund, 1888.	Authorised Issue.
		Subscribed.	Paid.		
		£	£	£	£
Bank of Ireland	1783	*2,769,231	2,769,231	1,034,000	3,738,428
Northern Banking Co.	1824	2,000,000	389,147	190,000	243,440
Hibernian Bank	1825	2,000,000	500,000	Nil.	—
Provincial Bank of Ireland	1825	4,080,000	540,000	174,000	927,667
Belfast Banking Co.	1827	2,000,000	400,000	349,272	281,611
National Bank.................	1835	7,500,000	1,500,000	241,889	852,269
Ulster Bank	1836	2,400,000	400,000	450,000	311,079
Royal Bank of Ireland	1836	1,500,000	300,000	200,000	—
Munster and Leinster Bank	1885	375,000	150,000	50,000	—

All the banks, with the exception of the Bank of Ireland, have adopted limited liability under the Act of 1882. The extent of the liability of the Bank of Ireland Stockholders would seem to be open to doubt. In the Charter nothing is stated on the subject, but a joint opinion was signed on February 26th, 1886, by Mr. (now Mr. Justice) Kekewich, Q.C., then standing counsel to the Bank of England, Sir Richard Webster, Q.C., now Attorney-General, and Mr. Hornell, to the effect that "the holders of Bank of Ireland Stock are not liable for any debts or engagements of the Bank."

---

* Equal to £3,000,000 Irish.

CHAPTER II.

IRISH COINAGE AND CURRENCY.*

Wealth of the people—Danish and Anglo-Saxon coinages—Issues of King John—Barter—Importation of foreign coin—Coinages of English Kings and Queens—The "Gun Money" of James II—Coinages of William III and Anne—Copper coinage of George II—Scarcity of subsidiary money—Scarcity of silver coin after the potato famine—Wood's halfpence and the Drapier letters.

IN the banking crises of the two preceding centuries the scarcity and depreciation of the coinage were important factors. It will be useful, therefore, to notice the various changes in the currency which have taken place, from the earliest times up to the present day.

It will, perhaps, surprise many people to hear that in art and literature, Ireland, in the fifth, sixth and seventh centuries was far in advance of England. This is shown by the beautifully illuminated manuscripts of those early periods which still exist, while the writings of the Venerable Bede, an Irishman who flourished towards the end of the seventh century, are superior to any other literary productions of his era.

But although the wealth of the people is evident from the abundance of ring money, torques and other ornaments belonging to those and earlier epochs, no coins are known until about the eighth or ninth century, when the first mint was erected by the Ostmen, or Danes, who had invaded the country.† Their coins, which are very rude, and were only current among themselves, are apparently copies

---

* By the courtesy of the authorities, the Author had the opportunity of inspecting the very complete collection of Early Irish Coins at the British Museum.

† Ledwich's Antiquities of Ireland, 1783.

of Anglo-Saxon coins of the same period, executed by workmen who did not understand the letters which they imitated by a series of simple strokes. An improvement, however, is to be observed in subsequent issues. Coins were also struck by native kings, Anlaf (A.D. 930) and Sithric (A.D. 994) which may be considered the earliest Irish specimens. They bear the legend ON . DVFLI. or ON . DYFLI. Dyflin, or Duflin, being the ancient name of Dublin. Other coins of Irish kings about this period are also extant.

A portion of the country was already subject to England under the Anglo-Saxon kings, and there are coins of Ethelred (886) struck at Dublin, and also of Eldred (948) and Edgar (959).* Those of Canute, struck at Dublin, are described as good coins for the period, and bear the legend "Gnut Rex Anglorum." After the Norman conquest there is no certain account of money being coined in Ireland until the reign of King John, in 1210, when John de Grey, Bishop of Norwich, who had been entrusted with the government of the country, caused pennies, halfpennies and farthings to be coined, of the same weight as those of England, and they were made current in the country by proclamation. But the circulation of money among the people at this time, and, indeed, up to the seventeenth century, must have been very limited in amount. "They exchange," wrote Campion in 1570, "by commutation of wares for the most part, and have utterly no coin stirring in any great lord's houses." We have evidence of the continued prevalence of barter at a still more recent date.

Edward I., on the Irish coins, added to his title of "Rex Angliæ" that of "Dominus Hiberniæ." During succeeding reigns a great scarcity of coin seems to have prevailed, and to remedy this, in 1476 an enactment was made to encourage the importation of foreign coin; the rider, fine and good, was to pass for five shillings, the ducat, the lyon, the crown, and the crusade, for the same amount, the Burgundy noble for ten shillings, the salute for five, and the halves and quarters in proportion. The gold noble was also raised in value, from ten to twelve shillings. At various other periods of Irish history, foreign gold and silver coins, especially Spanish, Portuguese and French, were in circulation at a value fixed by proclamation.

* Humphrey's Coin Collector's Manual, Vol. II., 1883.

From the time of Edward I. down to 1737, successive Sovereigns tinkered with the Irish coinage. Henry VIII. coined sixpences worth only fourpence in England. Queen Mary, while prohibiting the currency of base money in England, ordered, in 1553, base shillings, groats, and twopenny pieces to be struck for Ireland. Under Elizabeth the ounce of silver was cut into sixty, instead of twenty, pennies. During that Queen's reign, base coin of the nominal value of four thousand pounds, circulating in England, was called in and converted into eight thousand pounds in half shillings and groats, and this money was declared, by Her Majesty's proclamation, to be the lawful and current money of Ireland. It was further declared that if any person or persons should refuse it in any kind of traffic or trade, in the payment of wages, stipends, or debts, according to its valuation, they should be punished as contemners of Her Majesty's royal prerogative and commands. Further, to make the coin more current, it was ordered that all other moneys should be annulled, esteemed as bullion and not as the lawful money of the realm.*

James I. seems to have feebly attempted to regulate the currency, though he is said to have made an experimental issue of copper farthings, which, if they failed in England, might be sent to Ireland as pence and halfpence. He issued proclamations fixing the value of the base shillings, coined in the previous reign, first at fourpence, and afterwards at threepence. In 1604 he altered the inscription on his English and Irish coins from "King of England and Scotland" to "King of Great Britain and Ireland." In the time of Cromwell the issue of tokens by private individuals was permitted. These tokens were of brass or copper.

James II. does not appear to have interfered with the coinage until he landed in Dublin, in 1688, after his flight to France. In order that the few thousand livres borrowed from the French king might go the farther, he issued a proclamation increasing their value, but, as this expedient did not supply money fast enough, he opened mints at Dublin and Limerick for the issue of coins composed of brass and copper mixed, and this money was made legal tender for all debts whatever. As the mint could not go on without metal, the

* Simon's Irish Coins, 1749.

Master General of the Ordnance was ordered to deliver to the Commissioners of the Mint some old brass guns which were lying in the castle yard. Hence the name of "gun money" which was given to the coins. When the cannon was exhausted, its place was supplied by broken bells, old copper, and brass, and pewter kitchen utensils. The nominal amount of the base money thus coined is stated by Simon as £1,596,799 0*s.* 6*d.*, while the value of the material composing it was estimated at £6,495 8*s.* 4*d.*

The first act of William III. was to reduce the value of these brass crowns and halfcrowns, and they were ordered to pass at one penny each.

Queen Anne made several regulations respecting the currency, under one of which, the value of the new French Louis d'or was fixed at £1 2*s.* In the reign of George I. a proclamation was issued for making the new gold coin of Portugal current in Ireland, the large gold coin at £4 and the smaller ones in proportion. George II. was the first king who made a real attempt to place the Irish coinage on an equality with that of England, as in 1737 to remedy the scarcity of coin, he caused fifty tons of copper money to be issued of the same size and weight as the copper coin current in England.

In Carr's "Tour in Ireland" the following description is given of the currency in 1806 :—

1st. *A copious effusion of paper* from a guinea note to several thousand pounds.

2nd. *English guineas*, seldom seen out of the north of Ireland, worth £1 2*s.* 9*d.* each.

3rd. *Dollars*, worth five shillings and five pence Irish each.

4th. *Silver Bank Tokens* of six shillings Irish each.

5th. *Silver Bank Tokens* called tenpenny and fivepenny pieces, worth so much Irish each.

6th. *Hogs* or *Shillings*, sometimes called *thirteens*, worth thirteen pence Irish each.

7th. *Pigs* or testers, worth seven-pence Irish each.

8th. *Penny*, *halfpenny* and *farthing* pieces, a very recent coinage.

Wakefield, in his "Account of Ireland,"* published in 1812, says :—"In few countries in Europe has money been subjected to more changes in the same period, either by the admixture of bad metal or by alterations made in the nominal value of the different coins of which it was composed." The scarcity of subsidiary coinage was indeed a fruitful and always recurring source of grievance among Irish merchants, and the absolute dearth of silver and copper coins occasioned great inconvenience to traders. At one period, in 1737, silver was at a premium of from fourpence to sevenpence in the £, and the large disproportion in value between the gold and silver coins current in the kingdom further tended to reduce the circulation of silver. To remedy this evil, various schemes were proposed, and the Government at length decided that gold and silver should be brought nearly to a par by lowering the value of the dearer metal. A proclamation was issued on the subject by the Lords Justices and Council on the 29th September, 1737, by which the English guinea was fixed at £1 2*s.* 9*d.*, the half-guinea at 11*s.* 4½*d.*, the moidore was to pass for £1 9*s.* 3*d.*, the half for 14*s.* 8*d.*, the Spanish or French double pistole for £1 16*s.* 6*d.*, and the French Louis d'or for £1 2*s.* The coinage of Ireland was not finally assimilated to that of England until 1825, when an Act † was passed to remedy the complexity of accounts and other inconveniences arising from the difference of currencies. This Act recites that the English shilling was then accepted and paid in Ireland as thirteen pence, and enacts that the currency of Great Britain shall be the currency of the United Kingdom, and all receipts, payments and contracts were to be made in it.

A scarcity of silver coin experienced in more recent times may be worth relating. It occurred between May, 1846, and February, 1847, when the Inspectors of Government Works, instituted after the potato famine of 1845–1846, were unable to obtain sufficient silver to pay the wages of the labourers. Silver actually then commanded a premium of ten shillings per cent. It was suggested that the coin had been hoarded with a view to embarrass the Government, but a more reasonable solution is that the failure of the potato crop, by putting an end to the payment of rent in labour and kind, occasioned

* Vol. II., p. 160. † 6 Geo. IV., c. 79.

a demand for coin to fill the vacancy which the system of barter had hitherto supplied. One of the Inspectors writing from Skibbereen, on 6th December, 1846, said :—

"I have again reported to the Board the actual necessity of a large supply of silver being as speedily as possible forwarded to the Cork branch and made available to the branch here. The bank has issued for the service of the pay clerks upwards of £5,000 in one week, and there is no more. Whilst every obstruction is given to me to get silver, and a greater obstruction to my officers, what am I to do? I went round the town myself and begged it everywhere as an act of benevolence, and almost in every place or shop I was refused. Mr. L. was the only merchant-shopkeeper who gave me £15. Mr. S. the miller gave me £100 for the Sheepshead Road, whereon there are 1,200 people to be paid. Be pleased in your visit to His Excellency to impress the necessity of an immediate supply of silver, otherwise the works must be stopped. My officers will be torn to pieces. They already attempted a serious assault at the Sheepshead Road on the pay clerk, and it was then, in mercy, I obtained a hundred and odd pounds from Mr. S. the miller."

Silver was, however, afterwards brought into the country in such quantity, that the banks experienced difficulty in storing or using it.

But no account of the Irish coinage would be complete without some notice of Wood's halfpence and Dean Swift's celebrated "Drapier's Letters."

In 1723, there was an acknowledged deficiency of copper coin, and the king (George I.), in virtue of his prerogative, granted to a Mr. Wm. Wood a patent for coining farthings and halfpence to the nominal value of £108,000. The patent was procured for Wood through the influence of the Duchess of Kendal, and the anticipated profit, which would have amounted to about £40,000, was to be divided between the Duchess and the patentee. The new coins were admittedly superior in sterling value to the issues preceding them, but they were received with considerable dislike and suspicion. It was contended that the patent had been obtained by notorious misrepresentations, that the grant of patents for coining to private individuals was highly injurious, and that when the coinage was executed copper would become a fifth part of the entire specie currency.* Both

* "By the best computation the current coin of Ireland in gold, silver and copper is thought not to exceed £400,000." Letter of Dr. Boulter to the Duke of Newcastle, 14th January, 1724.

Houses of Parliament passed addresses to the Crown accusing Wood of fraud and deceit, and complaining that the terms of the patent were infringed both in quality and quantity. They also asserted that the circulation of the coins would be highly prejudicial to the revenue, destructive of the commerce, and of most dangerous consequences to the rights and properties of the subjects. No answer having been returned to these addresses, the two Houses passed resolutions that supplies should not be voted, and that their sittings should be suspended until some reply was obtained or the patent withdrawn. The king thereupon wrote expressing his regret that the patent was not acceptable to the Irish people, and promising an inquiry into the manner in which it had been carried out. Assuming, therefore, that the dispute was at an end, Parliament voted the required supplies, and replied that they were grateful for his Majesty's kindness. A Committee of inquiry was accordingly appointed, and an attempt was made to prove that the assertion of fraud was false, by means of an assay at the Mint under Sir Isaac Newton of a selection of the coins. So far as these specimens were concerned, the analysis showed that the terms of the patent had been adhered to, and to this effect the Committee reported. A copy of their report, with that of Sir Isaac Newton was sent to Dublin, and the issue of the coins recommenced. It was at this point that Dean Swift appeared on the scene as the defender of Irish liberty, a *rôle* which, on previous occasions, had brought him into collision with the Government of the day, and in a series of now famous letters, signed "M. B. Drapier," exhorted his countrymen to have nothing to do with the halfpence. He accused Wood, whom he described as "a mean ordinary man, a hardware dealer and a mechanic," but who appears to have been a large proprietor of iron and copper mines in England, of having bought up all the old copper in Ireland to create an artificial scarcity. "Let Wood," he said, "and his crew of founders and tinkers, coin on till there is not an old kettle left in the kingdom. By his own computation we are to pay three shillings for what is worth one. I will rather choose to be hanged than have all my substance taxed at the arbitrary will and pleasure of the venerable Mr. Wood." The "Drapier" arguments were obviously unsound and untenable, but they were not on this account less acceptable to the impressionable and unreasoning people to whom they were addressed, and on the publication of the first letter the popular excitement, already great, immensely increased. Wood was burned and hanged in effigy. The Viceroy made repeated efforts to procure from the king a withdrawal of the patent, but without avail. The Government offered a reward of £300 for the detection of the author of the letter; failing to discover him, the prosecution of the printer was ordered, but when the case came before the Grand Jury they threw out the bill. At length, all efforts to subdue the popular clamour having proved ineffectual, the patent was withdrawn, and Wood was compensated with a pension of £3,000 per annum for eight years.

CHAPTER III.

Early History of Irish Banking. The Private Banks.

Brokers—Goldsmiths—John Demar—Uncontrolled System of banking—Failures of Mead and Curtis, and of Burton and Falkiner—Dublin bankers in 1735—Failures of Willcocks and Dawson, of Dillon and Ferrall and of Lennox and French—Legislation—Panic in 1760—Failure of Clements, Malone, and Gore—History of La Touche and Company, Sir William Newcomen and Company and Finlay and Company—Action of the Irish Parliament—Bankers in Ireland in 1767—Panic in 1770—Causes of the disasters—Private Banking 1770–1783.

THOUGH the history proper of banking in Ireland commences with the establishment of the Bank of Ireland in 1783, a primitive system of private banking was carried on at a much earlier period. The bankers of that pre-historic time appear, however, more in the light of brokers or intermediaries, who brought borrowers and lenders together for a consideration, which was fixed by an Act of the Irish Parliament, passed in 1634,* at a maximum of five shillings per cent. for the original loan, and twelve pence per cent. for any renewal. It was enacted that if scriveners, brokers, solicitors, or drivers of bargains for contracts took any higher consideration, they were to forfeit £20, and to be imprisoned for half a year. The object of this Act was to restrain usury, and by it the legal rate of interest was restricted to ten per cent. per annum. It may be presumed that, in the opinion of the legislature, a borrower who was reckless enough to pay ten per cent., would not be likely to be very particular about the rate of brokerage, and hence the necessity of regulating the amount payable to "the driver of the bargain." The

* 10 Charles I., cap. 22.

The business of banking seems afterwards to have passed into the hands of the goldsmiths, tradesmen, and general dealers who carried it on in addition to their own callings. It consisted chiefly in the issue of promissory notes against the deposit of money, and the scarcity of specie would doubtless cause these notes to enter freely into circulation. Their status as negotiable instruments was not, however, legally defined until the year 1709,* when it was enacted that "to the intent to encourage trade and commerce which will be much advanced" thereby, these notes were to be assignable and transferable by endorsement. The business of banking was, evidently, a profitable one, judging from the number of persons engaged in it, even as far back as the end of the seventeenth century. Lawrence, in "The interest of Ireland in its Trade and Wealth stated" published in 1682, complains of the number of single banks or exchangers who failed within a few years, and estimates the damage they had caused at £50,000, which would of course be considered a very large sum in those days.

One of the earliest Irish bankers, of whom any trace exists, was John Demar or Damer. He had served under Cromwell during the Civil War, as captain of a troop of horse, and after the restoration of Charles II. he sold his landed property in the West of England and settled in Ireland. He carried on his business of a usurer at a well-known place of resort in Dublin, called "The London Tavern," where, according to Swift, "he touched the pence while others touched the pot." He died on 6th July, 1720, at No. 34, Smithfield, Dublin, at the ripe age of 92. Swift, with some of his usual party, happened to be at Mr. Sheridan's in Capel Street, when the news of Demar's death was brought to them, and the following elegy was the joint composition of the company:—

> "Know all men by these presents, Death, the tamer
> By mortgage, has secured the corpse of Demar;
> Nor can four hundred thousand sterling pound
> Redeem him from his prison under ground,
> His heirs might well, of all his wealth possess'd,
> Bestow to bury him one iron chest.

* 8 Anne, cap. 11.

Plutus, the god of wealth, will joy to know
His faithful steward in the Shades below.
He walk'd the streets, and wore a thread bare cloak;
He dined and supp'd at charge of other folk,
And by his looks, had he held out his palms,
He might be thought an object fit for alms.
So to the poor if he refused his pelf,
He used them full as kindly as himself.
Where'er he went, he never saw his betters;
Lords, knights, and squires, were all his humble debtors;
And under hand and seal, the Irish nation
Were forced to own to him their obligation.
He that could once have half a kingdom bought
In half a minute is not worth a groat.
His coffers from the coffin could not save
Nor all his interest keep him from the grave.
A golden monument would not be right,
Because we wish the earth upon him light.
Oh, London Tavern! thou hast lost a friend,
Though in thy walls he ne'er did farthing spend;
He touch'd the pence while others touch'd the pot;
The hand that signed the mortgage paid the shot.
Old as he was, no vulgar known disease
On him could ever boast a power to seize;
But, as he weigh'd his gold, grim Death in spite
Cast in his dart, which made three moidores light;
And, as he saw his darling money fail,
Blew his last breath to sink the lighter scale.
He, who so long was current, 'twould be strange
If he should now be cried down since his change.
The sexton shall green sods on thee bestow;
Alas, the sexton is thy banker now!
A dismal banker must that banker be,
Who gives no bills but of mortality."

The following epitaph on Demar is also from the pen of Swift:—

"Beneath this verdant hillock lies
Demar, the wealthy and the wise;
His heirs for winding sheet bestowed,
His money bags together sewed;
And that he might securely rest,
Have put his carcase in a chest.

> The very chest in which, they say,
> His other self, his money, lay.
> And if his heirs continue kind
> To that dear self he left behind
> I dare believe, that four in five
> Will think his better half alive."

Demar was never married, and nearly the whole of his great wealth passed to his nephew, John Demar or Damer, an ancestor of the Earls of Portarlington, whose family name is Dawson-Damer.

The Act of Parliament, passed in 1709, referred to on a preceding page, is entitled "An Act for the better payment of Bills of Exchange, and making Promissory Notes more obligatory," and gives power to protest inland, as well as foreign bills and promissory notes for non-acceptance or non-payment. It recites that "great damage and other inconveniences do frequently happen in the course of trade and commerce, by reason of delays of payment and other neglects," and this is by no means surprising. The business of banking was at that time perfectly free and uncontrolled; anyone was at liberty to issue not only bank notes, but also silver and copper coin; there was no bankrupt law, and in the event of liquidation, recourse to a special Act of Parliament was necessary, if the assets remaining were sufficient to meet the expenses attending such a costly proceeding. The House of Commons at that time supplied the need of a court of bankruptcy, hearing and adjudicating upon the petitions of creditors or of debtors seeking for relief.

But though there is evidence that the failures of private bankers were considerable in number, and that the aggregate amount of their deficiencies was very large, no record of a bank coming to grief is to be found in the proceedings of the Irish Parliament until the year 1731, when the Act 5 Geo. II., c. 23, was passed for the relief of the creditors of Mead and Curtis, a Dublin firm, established in 1716, and who suspended payment on the 14th June, 1727. The partners were James Mead and George Curtis; the latter died in October following the suspension. It is to be noted that, while the failure occurred in June, 1727, the parliamentary stage of the matter was not reached until March, 1731, during which interval John Rathborne, a merchant of the city of Dublin, appears to have been engaged in winding up the firm's affairs, and for this, his remuneration, fixed by the Act, was one shilling for each pound realised. When the case reached the House of Commons the progress was rapid enough. The Bill was read a second time on 4th March, a third time on 7th March, and it was sent to the Upper House on the 10th March, 1731.

Two years later, similar relief was granted to the creditors of Burton and Falkiner, also of Dublin, who commenced business in or about 1700, the style of the firm being then Burton and Harrison. For some time they seem to have been fairly prosperous, the partners being possessed of considerable landed property. But possessions of this kind did not always imply that the bankers were themselves wealthy. At that time, land constituted almost the only available investment for the surplus balances of customers, and the unrealisability of the security in time of panic was the cause of several failures. At the date of Harrison's death, in July, 1725, the firm evidently stood in high repute, as in "an elegy on the much lamented death of Mr. Harrison," published in Dublin, he is described as "the only Crœsus of the Banker's Race." After Harrison's death, Burton, the surviving partner, took his son and Daniel Falkiner into partnership. The liabilities of the firm, presided over by this "Banking Crœsus," then exceeded the assets by £65,173 4*s.* 6½*d.*, and the two Burtons bound themselves to Falkiner, in the penal sum of £100,000, to make good the deficit within six months, but this they failed to do. Benjamin Burton* died in May, 1728, and the business was continued by Samuel Burton and Falkiner until June 25th, 1733, when they stopped payment. The interests involved in their failure appear to have been of considerable magnitude, as their affairs were before the House of Commons, at frequent intervals, for a long period, and form the subject of several Acts of Parliament, the last Act† being dated 1757, nearly a quarter of a century after the failure took place. Burton and Falkiner acted as bankers to the Government. In the month of their failure, the Deputy Receiver and Paymaster-General lodged with them £4,842 5*s.* 2¼*d.* to be remitted to the Paymaster-General of Great Britain for the payment of Irish troops abroad, and

* Lord Mayor of Dublin in 1706.

† 31 George II., cap. 12.

at the time of the stoppage they still had part of this sum, £1,543 0*s.* 2¼*d.*, in their hands. The liquidators were empowered to repay this amount to the Deputy Receiver out of the first realisations.

In 1735 five banks were conducting business in Dublin, viz.:—

James Swift and Company, of Eustace Street, and afterwards of Castle Street.

Hugh Henry, of Upper Ormond Quay (afterwards succeeded by Henry Mitchell and Company).

Nuttall and McGuire, of Lower Ormond Quay.

La Touche and Kane, of Castle Street.

And Joseph Fade and Company, of Thomas Street.

After the failure of Burton and Falkiner, a lapse of over twenty years took place, and though it is recorded that during this interval failures were rife, and credit at its lowest ebb, the character of the defaulting institutions may be gauged by the fact that there is no further instance of parliamentary intervention until December, 1755, when the partners in the firm of Willcocks and Dawson joined their creditors in petitioning the House for relief. The bank was started by Joseph Fade. In 1728 he took John and Isachar Willcocks into partnership. The latter died in April, 1744, and Joseph Fade died in May, 1748, soon after which the surviving partner took John Dawson into partnership, and business was continued under the style of Willcocks and Dawson until March 1st, 1755, when the bank closed its doors, mainly owing to frauds on the part of their cashier, Richard Brewer. Brewer entered the service of the firm in 1736, and ten years later was in receipt of an annual salary of £80, which was increased, in 1750, to £100 per annum. He appears to have possessed the confidence of his employers, because, at the date of the stoppage, he was indebted to the bank in the sum of £70,245 11*s.* 7½*d.* which he was alleged to have abstracted and used in building and other speculations.

Less than a month later, in January, 1756, the House of Commons was occupied with the affairs of Dillon and Ferrall, who had suspended payment, and absconded, on March 6th, 1754, nearly a year prior to the collapse of Willcocks and Dawson. This bank was originally established by Theobald Dillon, and was carried on by him for many years in conjunction with his son Thomas, on the Inn's Quay, Dublin, under the style of Theobald Dillon and Son. Theobald Dillon died in 1736, and his son took Richard Ferrall into partnership in 1748, the latter bringing no capital into the business, and receiving an indemnity against loss. He seems to have introduced a good connection to the bank, but otherwise it must be allowed that the terms of partnership were very favourable to him; though it is difficult to see what value could be attached to an indemnity against loss given by one partner to another.

On 3rd March, 1755, two days only after the suspension of Willcocks and Dawson, the citizens of Dublin were startled by the announcement that the partners in the respectable firm of Lennox and French had absconded. This bank was opened in 1739, on the Ormond Quay, by William Lennox, who took George French into partnership in 1751. A number of other minor firms also disappeared about this time, without going through the formality of first meeting their engagements.

A commercial crisis was invariably followed then, as now, by the appointment of a select committee of the House of Commons, and accordingly a committee was directed to meet, to enquire into "the state of public credit, the causes of its decay, and how it may be restored." The committee reported that credit had suffered much by persons carrying on the business of bankers without sufficient capital, and recommended that restrictions should be placed on persons establishing themselves as such, by requiring them to register in the public registry such real and personal estate as they proposed to be a security to the public. It was also recommended that the names of issuing bankers should be stated on their notes, that bankers should not be permitted to trade as merchants, and that it was necessary to make it felony "without benefit of clergy," in cashiers or clerks to embezzle money exceeding £50 in amount. The committee also resolved "that the obliging bankers and their cashiers to cancel all notes at the time of payment, will contribute to preserve public credit." This resolution is somewhat difficult to understand, as the connection between the preservation of public credit and the cancelment of paid notes is not at all apparent. All these recommendations, except the first, which was by far the most important, and the last, were embodied in an Act passed in 1755.*

The Act did not, however, have its desired effect in the restoration of public credit, which continued to decline, failure succeeding failure until 1760, when the whole banking fabric of the country fell to the ground. In Dublin out of six banks, there were three failures, viz. :— Richard and Thomas Dawson of Jervis Street, Henry Mitchell and J. Macarell of Ormond Quay, and a banker named Clements, who was probably the Nathaniel Clements referred to below. In the meantime, also, another failure had been added to the list, viz. :—Clements, Malone, and Gore, a firm established on July 3rd, 1758, which, after a very brief career of four months, closed its doors on November 1st, 1758. The partners in this bank were the Right Honourables Nathaniel Clements and Anthony Malone and Mr. John Gore. They issued deposit notes payable to bearer at seven days' notice, with interest at the rate of tenpence per week for every £100 (= $2\frac{1}{6}$ per cent.), the money thus obtained, and it seems that the amount deposited greatly exceeded the expectations of the bankers, being invested in land or on loan at 5 per cent. Four months only, after their establishment the depositors began to demand repayment of their notes, and the loans and land securities not being immediately realisable, the bank had to stop payment.

They afterwards submitted a proposal to their creditors offering promissory notes, bearing interest at the rate of six per cent. per annum until paid, in discharge of their liabilities, and these terms were accepted by a majority of the creditors. The estates of the partners were settled on trustees for purpose of sale, and the trustees were empowered, as often as they raised a sum of £5,000 or upwards, in excess of the interest on the outstanding notes, which was accorded priority of payment, to apply the amount in liquidation of the notes—the order of the claimants being decided by ballot.

An amusing lampoon was published in Dublin after the failure of this firm. It is entitled "The New Bankers proved Bankrupts, in a Dialogue between themselves and a Free Citizen," and is in the form of a supposed dialogue between the partners "Toney, Natey and

* 29 George II., cap. 16.

Gorey," and an importunate depositor. The depositor asks for his money, and, failing to obtain it, taxes the bankers with having stopped payment. They reply by reminding him that he is in the presence of two Privy Counsellors and a lawyer as well as a banker, but, they add, "What breeding can we expect in a vulgar citizen?" The Right Honourable Anthony Malone is made to say "Do you know, sir, who I am? that I am a Prop of the Laws? and a gentleman? As such it lieth in my power to punish offences offered to *our* Person." But subsequently, after some strong language on both sides, he is made to admit his guilt. He confesses that the depositor's money was employed to clear off encumbrances on his own estates, and he concludes by singing a song "against all cutpurses," in which unenviable company he is made to include himself. The allegation that the funds of the depositors were wholly employed for the debtor's own purposes, seems, however, to be at variance with the facts, as the statement of affairs disclosed very considerable, though unrealisable, assets.

The three remaining banks in Dublin were, La Touche and Co., Thomas Gleadowe and Co., and Thomas Finlay and Co.

Messrs. La Touche and Co. commenced business in 1725, as La Touche and Kane. Nathaniel Kane, the partner, was Lord Mayor in 1734, and had been accused by Dr. Lucas, M.P., of appropriating some of the city funds, but successfully vindicated himself.* Their bank was moved in 1735 to the house, built by David La Touche, junior, son of the founder of the firm, in which the business was carried on until 1871, when it was absorbed by the Munster Bank. Five members of the La Touche family had seats in Parliament in 1800, and only one voted for the Union. La Touche and Co. were the "Coutts'" of Dublin. They were the bankers of all the Irish nobility and gentry, and it may be said that almost the entire wealth of the country was concentrated in their hands. The removal of the parliamentary representation to Westminster would, necessarily, mean the loss of many valuable accounts. Few firms have enjoyed higher repute. They were agents for Coutts and Co., and Ransom Bouverie and Co., of London; for Pybus Call and Co. and Puget; for George

---

* The History and Practice of Banking by C. M. Collins.

Newenham and Co., Pike, and Hewitt of Cork; for Alderman Simon Newport of Waterford, and many other firms.

Thomas Gleadowe and Co., afterwards Sir William Gleadowe-Newcomen and Co., started business at Castle Street, in 1746, in succession to James Swift and Co. They removed in 1777 to 19, Mary's Abbey, returning to Castle Street in 1781, to the building afterwards occupied by the Hibernian Bank. In 1770, William Gleadowe, then the head of the firm, assumed the name of Newcomen on his marriage to a lady of that name, and was created a baronet in 1781. In 1800 he was rewarded for his vote in Parliament, in favour of the Union, by a grant of £20,000, and his wife was raised to the dignity of a peeress, with the title of Baroness Newcomen. She subsequently, in 1803, became Viscountess Newcomen. The partners in 1799 were, Sir William Gleadowe-Newcomen, Bart., Thomas Gleadowe-Newcomen and Arthur Dawson.

Thomas Finlay and Co. were in existence some time before 1760, and came to grief in 1835 or 1836. The partners in 1767 were Thomas Finlay, Art Jones Nevill, Ben Geale, and John Hunt.*

But although these three banks still kept their doors open, they refused to discount bills, and, in fact, almost suspended the transaction of business. The merchants of Dublin held a meeting in April, 1760, at which the difficulties of the situation were considered and deplored. As the result of this meeting a petition was presented to the House of Commons setting forth "the low state to which public and private credit has been of late reduced in this kingdom, and particularly in this city, of which the successive failures of so many banks and private traders in different parts of the kingdom, in so short a time as since October last, are incontestable proofs," and that the petitioners had "repeatedly attempted to support the sinking credit of the kingdom by association and otherwise, and are satisfied that no resource is now left but what may be expected from the wisdom of Parliament to avert the calamities with which this kingdom is at present threatened."

A committee of inquiry was again appointed by the House, and on April 23rd, 1760, reported that the quantity of paper in circulation

* Wilson's Dublin Directory for 1767.

(due presumably to the numerous failures) was insufficient to support the trade and manufactures of the kingdom. On the recommendation of the committee, Parliament, with a view to "re-establish credit and quiet the minds of the people at this critical and distrustful season," undertook to support the three surviving banks to the extent of £50,000 each, thus in some measure allaying the general distress. The notes of these bankers were also authorised to be received as cash from the subscribers to a loan then in course of being raised.

In 1767, according to the "Gentleman's and Citizen's Almanack," published in Dublin, there were the following bankers in Ireland :—

Dublin.

Messrs. William Gleadowe and Co., Castle Street.
Messrs. David La Touche and Son, Castle Street.
Messrs. Thomas Finlay and Co., Upper Ormond Quay.
Messrs. Sir George Colebrooke, Bart., and Co., Mary's Abbey.

Hours of attendance 10 to 3.

Cork.

Messrs. Rogers, Travers and Sheares, Hamon's Marsh.
Messrs. Falkiner and Mills, near the Custom House.

Hours of attendance from 10 to 12, and from 4 to 6, and on Tuesdays and Fridays at five in the evening, for post business only. Holidays—January 1st, Good Friday, Easter Monday and Tuesday, Whit-Monday and Tuesday, December 25th, 26th, 27th, and 28th.

Waterford.

Alderman Simon Newport.

Sir George Colebrook, Bart., and Co., mentioned in the above list, were London bankers, dating from about 1720–1721, and they opened a branch in Mary's Abbey, Dublin, in 1764. Their suspension in 1770 was the cause of another panic, so intense, that the Lord Lieutenant and some of the nobility and gentry issued a notice pledging themselves to receive the notes of the then existing Dublin bankers, viz., La Touche and Co., Gleadowe-Newcomen and Co., Dawson, Coates and Lawless, and Finlay and Co.

Various reasons, and many economic fallacies, were adduced to account for these disasters. It was contended that the banks had failed not from want of property, but from want of coin, and one writer asserts that the coal trade with England, which was then settled in coin, and was estimated at £60,000 per annum, was the principal cause of the drain of gold. Other authorities point to the rapid growth of the public debt, and the profligate expenditure of the government as a main cause of the evil. But the more probable cause of this wholesale demolition of the private banks is to be found in the disturbed condition and universal corruption of the country at this period. There can hardly be said to have been any government whatever. Parliament met seldom, and at irregular intervals. The Viceroy resided in the capital for only six months out of two years, and in his absence the reins of government were held by the Lord Justices, who were not usually chosen for the uprightness of their character or the excellence of their reputation. The tenure of land was insecure. The restraints on trade were injurious and vexatious. Whiteboys, cattle houghers, and midnight robbers ravaged the country, murdering people, killing and torturing cattle, and burning houses, in defiance of half-hearted efforts to secure peace and order. The restrictions on the Roman Catholics were severe, and provocative of intrigue and conspiracy. Absenteeism, due mainly to the political insecurity of the country, was then, as now, the stock grievance of Ireland. Following the example of the Viceroy, the nobility and gentry spent abroad the income derived from their Irish estates, and even the bishops lived in England, and openly sold their preferments. In high places, jobbery and corruption, and even peculation prevailed. Seats in Parliament were bought and sold, the buyer recouping himself by the sale of his vote in the House. Government sinecures and pensions secured on the revenues of Ireland, were bestowed on place hunters and favourites of the English Court. Can it then be wondered that the banks shared in this general insecurity and corruption? Moreover, the legal restriction imposed on bankers * making void as against creditors all conveyances to their children, even for a valuable consideration, prevented capitalists from

* 33 George II., cap. 14.

embarking in the business. In 1858, Mr. W. D. La Touche, in his evidence before the Select Committee of the House of Commons on the Bank Act, complained of the continuance of this antiquated restriction, and the Committee commented upon it in their Report.

From the year 1770 to 1797 private banking continued to decline. In Dublin, La Touche's, Sir Wm. Newcomen's, and Finlay's still remained; in Waterford Sir John Newport survived, and there were also banks in Cork, Clonmel, and Limerick. The country may possibly have been under-banked, but there was an absence of anything like panic or crisis. No new banks entered the field during the interval. Up to 1783 the want of confidence, produced by previous disasters, probably acted as a deterrent. After 1783 the competition and privileges of the Bank of Ireland would tend to discourage any new enterprise in the same direction.

CHAPTER IV.

Private Banks—*continued.*

Renewed formation of private banks—Numbers in 1797-1804—Registered bankers in Ireland in 1804—Issuers of I. O. U.'s—The Saddler-banker of Killarney—Means taken by the bankers to circulate notes—Numbers in 1804-1815—List of Banks drawing on London in 1817—Confidence shown in the banks—Liabilities of failed firms—Absence of circulating medium—Base coin in circulation—Absorption of private by Joint Stock Banks—Decline and ultimate extinction of private banking.

A RENEWED impetus was given to the formation of private banks in 1797, by the Bank Restriction Act, under which the Bank of Ireland was prohibited from making any payments in coin. This led to largely increased issues on the part of the Bank, and was accompanied by a corresponding increase in the issues of private banks. These mushroom concerns again began to spring up all over the country, existing only, it would seem, for the purpose of issuing notes, and closing their doors when the repayment of their obligations was demanded. Previously to 1797, as we have seen, there were few banks carrying on business outside Dublin, and the whole number in Ireland cannot then have exceeded a dozen. Between 1797 and 1800 several were established and failed, leaving eleven in existence in the latter year. In 1801, according to a Parliamentary Report issued in 1804,* the number had increased to twenty-three; in 1802 to twenty-nine, and in 1803 to thirty. The same authority gives the number in 1804 as

* Report of the House of Commons Committee on Circulating Paper, Specie and Current Coin in Ireland, 1804.

forty, but the following list of registered bankers compiled from information contained in the appendix to the Report, contains the names of fifty firms, presumably carrying on business, and in addition, there were probably a number of bankers whose names were not registered.

Dublin.

The Right Hon. David Latouche, John Latouche, Peter Latouche, and William Digges Latouche.

Sir William Gleadowe-Newcomen, Bart., Arthur Dawson, and Thomas Gleadowe-Newcomen.

John Finlay, John Lynam, John Geale, and Robert Law.

John Claudius Beresford, James Woodmason, and James Farrell.

Sir Thomas Lighton, Bart., Thomas Needham and Robert Shaw.

William Williams and Michael Finn.

Waterford.

Simon Newport, Sir John Newport, Bart., and William Newport.

John O'Neill.

Limerick.

Thomas Maunsell and Robert Maunsell.

Thomas Roche and William Roche.

Michael Furnell, Mathias Woodmason, and Henry Bevan.

Cork.

Stephen and James Roche.

Sir James Lawrence Cotter, Bart., Richard Kellett, Sir Richard Kellett, Knt., and William Augustus Kellett.

Joseph Pike.

George Newenham, George Newenham, jun., and John Leckey.

Sir Thomas Roberts, Bart., James Bonwell, and John Leslie.

Wexford.

Thomas Redmond and Matthew Widdup.

Richard Codd, jun., and Company.

Thomas Cullimore.

Robert Sparrow.

James Carpenter.

N. C. H. Hatchell.

John Redmond.

Enniscorthy.

Robert Woodcock.

Clementine Codd and Company.

William Sparrow.

New Ross.

George and Peter Roe.
John Rossiter and Company.
John Colclough, John Berkeley Deane, and Thomas Macleord.

Dungarvan.

James Buckley and Company.
James Fallow.

Kilkenny.

William Williams and Michael Finn (also at Dublin).
Conl. Loughnan and John Helsham.

Clonmel.

Solomon Watson, John Watson, and William Watson.

Athy.

Lewis Mansergh.

Fermoy.

John Anderson.

Mallow.

Robert Delacour and Hill Galwey.

Birr.

Thomas Bernard, Simpson Hackett. Richard Kearney, and William Hackett.

Rathdrum.

William Manning, jun.

Callan.

Michael Hearn.

Galway.

Walter Joyce and Mark Lynch.

Laughlin Bridge.

James Blacker and James Rawson.

Malahide.

Richard Wogan Talbot, and Edward Glascock.

Carlow.

John Bennett, Thomas Macartney, Thomas Bernard and Henry Macartney.

Wicklow.

Perrin and McDowell.

Tipperary.

James Scully and James Scully, jun.

Charleville.

Eyre Evans, Jonathan Bruce, and William Roberts.

Thomastown.

Robert Langrishe and Anthony Graves.

Londonderry.

Sir Andrew Ferguson, Bart., Henry Alexander, and John Bond.

This list is not inclusive of the numerous issuers of notes for small and broken amounts, consisting simply of an I. O. U. over a signature, which were put into circulation by any traders, or persons, who, to use the words of a witness before one of the Select Committees, "wanted to raise the wind." The following list extracted from the Parliamentary Report before referred to, of the seventy issuers of I. O. U.'s, in the district of Youghal alone, will sufficiently indicate their numbers and position, as well as their ability to pay their notes on demand. The notes varied in nominal amount from 3½*d.* to 6*s.* each.

"*In Youghal.*—10 grocers, 3 general shopkeepers, 1 stationer, 1 chandler, 1 hardware shopkeeper, 2 bakers, 1 corn factor, 1 cabinet maker, 1 shoemaker, 1 linen draper, 1 wool comber, 1 firm of registered bankers (G. and R. Giles).

"*In Castlemarty.*—2 grocers, 1 apothecary.

"*In Cloyne.*—4 grocers, 4 spirit retailers, 1 linen draper, 1 baker, 1 strong water retailer.

"*In Rostillan.*—1 miller.

"*In Whitegate.*—1 clerk to a corn factor.

"*In Middleton.*—1 cloth manufacturer, 1 maltster, 1 brewer, 1 corn merchant, 1 tobacco manufacturer, 2 shopkeepers, 1 grocer.

"*In Mallow.*—3 general shopkeepers, 1 baker, 2 innkeepers, 2 wool combers, 1 miller, 1 tanner.

"*In Dungarvan.*—5 corn merchants.

"*In Cappoquin.*—4 corn merchants.

"*In Lismore.*—1 shopkeeper.

"*In Clashmore.*—2 spirit retailers."

An amusing anecdote is related of one of these so-called bankers, a small saddler in Killarney, whose whole stock-in-trade and capital combined would probably not have produced forty shillings. A party of English tourists, before leaving the town, wished to exchange the saddler's notes for more negotiable paper, and accordingly paid a visit to his shop, where they found him hard at work making a saddle. One of the party addressed him thus :—

"Good morning to you, Sir! I presume you are the gentleman of the house?"

"At your service, ladies and gentlemen," returned the saddler.

"It is here, I understand, where the bank is kept?" continued the speaker.

"You are just right," replied the mechanic, "this is the Killarney Bank for want of a better."

The tourist then said "We are on the eve of quitting your town, and as we have some few of your notes which will be no manner of use to us elsewhere, I will thank you for cash for them."

The banker replied "Cash! plase your honour, what is that? Is it anything in the leather line? I have a beautiful saddle here, as ever was put across a horse; good and chape, upon my say so. How much of my notes have you, Sir, if you plase?"

The tourist counted out sixteen notes for various amounts, from 3*d.* to 3*s.* 9½*d.*, the total being 15*s.* 9*d.*

"I should be sorry, most noble," returned the banker, "to waste any more of your lordship's time, or of those sweet beautiful ladies and gentlemen; but I have an illigant bridle here, as isn't to be matched in Yoorup, Aishy, Afrikey or Merikey. Its lowest price is 15*s.* 6½*d.*, we'll say 15*s.* 6*d.* to yer lordship. If ye'll be plased to accept of it, there will be 2½*d.* or a 3*d.* note coming to your lordship and that will close the business at once."

The bankers adopted every possible means of securing a circulation for their generally unredeemable promises to pay. They attended fairs and market places for the purpose of exchanging their notes for coin, or for the notes of the Bank of Ireland. One instance is on record,* and it is by no means an isolated one of its kind, of a banker having entered into an arrangement with the paymaster of a regiment, to whom he agreed to give a percentage on such of his notes as he should force into circulation, by making them the medium of payment to the troops under his command, the percentage to be proportioned to the distance of the place where the notes were paid away from that where they were issued.

But, of the fifty or more banks existing in 1804, only nineteen remained in 1812, though in the latter year there were still thirty-three in operation. In 1815 the number became reduced to thirty-one,

* Marquis of Lansdowne's Speech in the House of Commons.

including six in Dublin. The London Post Office Directory of 1817 gives the following list of Irish Banks then drawing on London :—

Belfast	...	...	Gordon and Company.
"	...	...	H. Montgomery and Company (Northern Bank).
Clonmel	...	...	W. Riall and Brothers.
Cork	...	...	Sir W. Roberts and Company.
"	...	...	G. Newenham and Company.
"	...	...	Joseph Pike.
"	...	...	S. and J. Roche.
Dublin	...	...	Sir T. G. Newcomen and Company.
"	...	...	Hon. D. Latouche and Company.
"	...	...	T. Finlay and Company.
"	...	...	B. Ball and Company.
"	...	...	R. Shaw and Company.
"	...	...	Sir W. A. Barr and Company.
Limerick	...	...	G. E. Bruce and Company.
"	...	...	T. and W. Roche.
"	...	...	Maunsell, Kennedy and Company.
Lurgan	...	...	Malcolmson and Company.
Mallow	...	...	De la Cour and Galway.
Waterford	...	...	R. and H. Hunt and Company.
"	...	...	W. Newport and Company.
Wexford	...	...	N. C. H. Hatchett.

After 1812 the ranks gradually thinned until 1820, when no less than eleven banks were swept away and only six were left standing.

The confidence placed in the banks is shown by the large liabilities they contrived to build up. Sir John Newport, in his evidence before the Select Committee of the House of Lords, in 1826, stated that the firm of Williams and Finn, of Dublin, had a note circulation of between £200,000 and £300,000, though at no time had they been worth £1,000. The liabilities of Colclough and Co., of New Ross (then a small town, but supporting four banks), were estimated at £200,000. Sir James Cotter and Co., of Cork, failed for £420,000. The active circulation of S. and J. Roche and Co., of Cork, in June, 1813, was about £300,000. The liabilities of Alexander's Bank, at Dublin, amounted to £500,000. Some of the defaulting institutions paid dividends,* one of 10s. in the £, and another of 5s., but others,

* Evidence of Mr. J Roche, before House of Lords Committee, 1826

and by far the greater number, paid nothing at all. A few resumed business, only to fail again later on.

The contraction in the circulating medium, caused by the diminution in the number of issuing bankers, again gave rise to great distress. In the towns in the South of Ireland, the people were actually in a state of starvation. The food which the country people were in the habit of bringing in was quite withdrawn. No supplies could be obtained, for, as no money remained, food brought into the towns was liable to be seized without payment. An incident is recorded of a five pound note being offered in Cork for a leg of lamb, and refused. In the provinces, even the notes of the Bank of Ireland were unnegotiable. No gold or silver was to be had, and credit of any kind was not procurable. In Limerick, a country gentleman, with an income of £1,500 per annum, had sent out invitations for a dinner party, and the same week the banks stopped payment. He, however, considered himself fortunate on finding in his purse a Bank of Ireland note for £10. No one doubted that the note was a good one, but no one could give change for it. Ten pounds in gold or silver were not in the country, and as for credit there was none to be had. In this extremity, with money which was not money, and without credit, having tried butcher, baker, and confectioner in vain, the gentleman gave up the idea of his dinner party in despair, and wrote to his friends to keep the engagement standing until he could procure cash or credit for a ten pound note.

In consequence of the over-issue of paper money, it was greatly depreciated in value, and the silver currency of the country becoming more valuable in the shape of bullion, was melted down and exported. In Dublin, base silver coin was privately manufactured and circulated in considerable quantities. Mr. W. Colville, a director of the Bank of Ireland, in his evidence before the House of Commons Committee, in 1804, said that during the previous five years there had been no silver in circulation, except a base coinage, one shilling of which, on an average, was worth sixpence. So defective was the copper money that not a single standard coin was said to be in circulation. The retail dealers refused to receive them, and buyers, who could afford it, allowed their purchases to amount to a guinea note, and then paid their indebtedness. The distress was, however,

D 2

chiefly in the south of Ireland. In the north, a people more thrifty and less simple, maintained a circulation of guineas, and paper was not current to anything like the same extent.

It might have been expected that the Irish would have learned a lesson of caution from the financial crises of earlier periods, and it is certainly surprising to find that their confidence in the banks was so little shaken. Mr. J. McNamara, in his evidence before the Committee of 1826, said: "The country people were afraid of gold, because they were not assured whether it was gold or not; they are not furnished with scales, they cannot weigh it, but if they are furnished with a note the person giving it puts his name upon it, and that gives them an assurance."

The passing of the Acts of 1820–1825, by permitting the establishment of joint stock banks, sounded the death-knell of private banking in Ireland. Some of the few remaining firms failed or discontinued; others merged into joint stock institutions. Thus the business of Sir Robert Shaw and Co., was transferred to the Royal Bank, of Messrs. Scully to the Tipperary Bank, of Messrs. Robert Gray and Co., to the English and Irish Bank, and of Messrs. Montgomery, of Belfast, to the Northern Bank. The Belfast Bank, a private institution, adopted the joint stock principle, with the same title. More recently, in 1878, Messrs. La Touche's old-established business was transferred to the Munster Bank, and Messrs. Ball retired in 1888 in favour of the Northern Bank, leaving only two firms in business, viz.: Messrs. Boyle, Low, Murray and Co., and Messrs. Guinness, Mahon and Co., both of Dublin, neither of whom have any power of issue. Nor is their business confined to banking. The last-named firm are also land agents, while Messrs. Boyle, Low, Murray and Co., are notaries and stock-brokers.

The history of private banking in the sister isle may thus be said to be virtually concluded. The rise and decline of the private banks constitutes a distinct epoch in Irish banking, terminating in the advent of the joint stock banks. The losses inflicted on the country by the failures of these moribund institutions may be fairly said to be unparalleled in the annals of any other nation, and Ireland has not, perhaps, even yet retrieved the injuries her commerce sustained from them.

CHAPTER V.

The Bank of Ireland.

Projected establishment of the Bank in 1695—Revival of the project in 1720—Action of the House of Commons in regard to it—Efforts of the promoters to secure subscriptions—Counter project of Lord Forbes—Rejection of the Bank Bill—Resolution of the House—Tract published by John Harding—Poem entitled "The Bank thrown down"—Reasons for the action of the House—Social and commercial progress of the country—The empty treasury—The Bank scheme again revived in 1782—The discussion in the House—Success of the measure—Terms of the Charter—First Governor and Directors—Legal rates of interest—Progress of the Bank—Provision as to the religion of Directors—Premises of the Bank—Renewals of the Charter—Suspension of cash payments in 1797—Note circulation 1797-1825—Dividends and bonus, 1783-1836—Partial withdrawal of privileges by 1 and 2 George IV., and subsequent Acts—Stamp duties on notes—Litigation with the Provincial Bank as to payment of notes in Dublin—Compromise between the two banks, and legislation resulting—Withdrawal of remaining privileges by Act 8 and 9 Victoria.

THE repeated failures of the private banks, and the ruin and distress which they entailed upon the community, the want of banking accommodation, and, above all, the scarcity of circulating media, created an urgent demand for a bank established on a secure and permanent basis, which would inspire the confidence of its constituents. But the scheme, which matured in the establishment of the Bank of Ireland, in 1783, took many years to ripen. Nearly a century before, in 1695, a number of the principal merchants of Dublin, animated by the success attending the establishment of the Bank of Scotland, called a meeting, with a view to forming a bank in Ireland on similar lines. A memorial was presented to the House of Commons on 17th of September in that year, setting forth "that the substance of the country was being miserably wasted by war, the laws of England, and the drain of specie," and recommending the establishment "of a public bank, or a fund of credit, for the encouragement of trade, and supply of the present want of money," to the favour of the House. The petition was referred to the Committee of Trade, and there the matter apparently ended, as no Report was subsequently made on it to the House.

Again, in 1720, after a period of severe commercial distress, the movement was revived under the powerful auspices of Lord Abercorn, Lord Boyne, and others, who petitioned the king (George I.) "in view of the great scarcity of coin which every day increased, and the general interruption of all matters of commerce which such a scarcity must necessarily occasion," for permission to start a public bank with a capital of £500,000. The Lords Justices having reported in favour of the scheme, the king authorised the Lord-Lieutenant to grant a commission and charter to erect a bank, leaving the House of Commons to settle the heads of a Bill to be submitted to them with this object. The project was also recommended to the notice of Parliament by the Duke of Bolton, the then Viceroy, in his speech from the throne in 1721. Accordingly, on September 21st, 1721, the House resolved itself into a committee to consider the question, and on September 29th they passed the following resolution :—"That it is the opinion of this committee that the establishing of a public bank upon a solid and good foundation, under proper regulations and restrictions, will greatly contribute to the restoring of credit and support of the trade and manufactures of this kingdom." Leave was then given to bring in the heads of a Bill upon the said resolution, and at a subsequent sitting (November 7th) the House resolved "that the commissioners in taking subscriptions pursuant to his Majesty's commission in order to erect a bank, have therein acted according to law, and pursuant to the trust reposed in them."

Meanwhile, however, it was seen that, notwithstanding the great efforts which had doubtless been made to obtain the required capital, the sense of the public was evidently opposed to the project. It is even said that the promoters resorted to the device of hiring carriages to block up the entrance to the bank, in order to encourage the idea that the subscription list was being rapidly filled up ; and Swift accuses them of having issued a list of subscribers which he alleges to have been "cooked." At this juncture,ies propounded, to appeared, revealing the jobbery and corruption ins'n regard to the operations of that period. Lord Forbes and others authority that the more ambitious project of a bank with a capital ction by which and a monopoly of the banking business of the country,es it to the the pill, they are stated to have offered a bribe of £50,000 ited in all of the House to secure their votes. the igno-

On December 9th, 1721, the special committee appointed tit of the the heads of the Bill, brought up their Report, and the House,pinion closed doors, and great solemnity, rejected the measure by a majorand of nearly two to one,* at the same time passing the following resolutions :—

"That this House, after long and mature deliberation, cannot find any safe foundation for establishing a public bank so as to render it beneficial to the kingdom.

"That the erecting or establishing a public bank in this kingdom will be of the most dangerous and fatal consequence to his Majesty's service and the trade and liberties of this nation.

"That an humble address be presented to his Majesty returning his Majesty the most sincere thanks of this House for his great goodness and condescension in leaving the consideration of establishing a bank in this kingdom to the wisdom of Parliament, assuring his Majesty that this House, after long and mature deliberation, cannot find any safe foundation for establishing the same so as to be beneficial to this nation, and representing the humble petition of this House that the erecting of this bank will be of dangerous and evil consequence to his Majesty's service and the welfare and liberty of this kingdom, and humbly to beseech his Majesty out of his tender concern for the good of all his subjects that he will be graciously pleased to give such directions to prevent the erecting of any bank as his Majesty in his great wisdom and goodness shall think proper."

And to mark their distrust of the scheme they further resolved :—

"That if any member of this House, or Commoner of Ireland, shall presume to solicit or endeavour to procure any grant, or get the Great Seal put to any charter for erecting a public bank in this

* 80 to 150. *Journal of the Irish House of Commons*, 1721.

the drain of speci-o the declared sense and resolutions of this House, public bank, or a -ir highest displeasure, and be deemed to act in con- supply of the pr-hority of this House, and an enemy to his country." The petition w-ber 11th, the House, being informed that a printed matter appar-en published by John Harding, entitled, "The last speech to the Hou words of the Bank of Ireland, which was executed in Again reen, on Saturday, the 9th inst.," containing great reflections moveme-proceedings of this House, it was resolved "that the said Lord -d paper was a false, scandalous and malicious libel, highly of -ecting on the justice and honour of the House," and the printer, John Harding, was ordered to be taken into the custody of the Sergeant-at-Arms. A Committee was appointed to enquire as to the authorship of the paper, but no further proceedings in the matter are recorded. Harding evidently continued in business until his death in April, 1725. It will be remembered that his prosecution was also ordered after the publication of the Drapier Letters, and he was known as "the Drapier's printer." His epitaph runs thus :—

"Here lies an honest man interred,
By merit and by chance preferred,
No friend to Wood, as wise as brave,
Though now he's level with the grave.
The 'Drapier's printer' was he styled
While stout Snarlerus he beguiled."

The following is an extract from a poem circulated in Dublin at the time, entitled "The Bank thrown down—to an excellent new tune" :—

This Bank is to make us a New Paper Mill
This Paper, they say, by the Help of a Quill
The whole Nation's Pockets with Money will fill
But we doubt that our Purses will quickly grow lank
If nothing but Paper comes out of this Bank.

Oh ! then to see how the Beggars will Vapour
For Beggars have Rags, and Rags will make Paper
And Paper makes Money, and what can be cheaper
Methinks I now see them, so jovial and crank
All riding on Horseback to "——" and the Bank.

Various reasons are assigned, and various theories propounded, to account for the action of the House of Commons in regard to the rejection of the Bank Bill. It is suggested by one authority that the Commons were alarmed at the bribery and corruption by which the scheme had been tainted. Sir John Sinclair attributes it to the terror which the failure of the South Sea scheme had excited in all the neighbouring countries.* Other writers ascribe it to the ignorance, not only of the majority of the House of Commons, but of the whole Irish nation ; and it must be allowed that the popular opinion of the time so far as it is exhibited by tracts and publications, and even by the utterances of the wisdom of the country in Parliament assembled, points to a considerable want of comprehension on subjects of currency and finance. The project was denounced by one writer as a means of circulating paper without money.† Swift urged that as the proposed bank would be a Protestant institution, "it may drain the greater part of the species of money from the Protestants, and leave them in lieu thereof, only paper, which can be of no effect in times of confusion, either for their defence or their subsistence, and consequently the ready money which must be allowed the sinews of war, being in the hands of the Irish papists may render them more formidable upon such a juncture to the English Protestant interest." ‡ There is, however, in addition to the apathy of subscribers, another solution, which is more acceptable. The Irish Parliament had always vigorously insisted on originating their own measures, and frequent illustration of their tenacity on this point is to be found in Irish history. In the present case, the Duke of Abercorn's petition had been made direct to the King. Parliament does not appear to have been previously consulted. It is not unlikely that they considered their dignity offended, and they resented it after their usual manner.

But though it is difficult, at this distance of time, to accurately estimate the value of the objections raised by the House of Commons,

---

* History of the Revenue," Vol. III.

† "Commercial Restraints of Ireland Considered," page 41.

‡ The Eyes of Ireland open, Being a short view of the project for establishing the intended Bank of Ireland.—Dublin, 1721.

it is clear that the distrust of the scheme was not confined to the House alone. Some idea of the feeling against it may be gathered from the fact that for upwards of half a century the project remained in abeyance. It was not until 1782 that the scheme was again put in motion. Events, in the meanwhile had been steadily moving in the direction of a public bank. The Test Act was repealed in 1780, and the disabilities under which the Roman Catholics laboured, were to some extent removed. In 1779 partial free trade was established. Before the Bank Act was passed, the Constitution of 1782 had become an accomplished fact. In the language of Grattan, Ireland had at last become a nation. A public bank was a necessary corollary of the removal of trade restrictions, and the realisation of the national aspirations. The country seemed indeed to be entering on a new era of prosperity. The linen trade in Ulster, and the fishing industry of the coast, two staple elements of Irish commerce, showed signs of revival, and agricultural produce rose in price. But the Treasury was empty. Messrs. La Touche had already advanced £20,000, and when still more funds were required to meet pressing demands, a second application to them had proved ineffectual. The success achieved by the Banks of England and Scotland began to attract attention, and the advantages to its budding commerce to a similar institution in Ireland became more and more obvious. Grateful for so ready a means of tiding over their financial difficulties, the Government in the Session of 1782, sanctioned the introduction into Parliament of a Bill for the erection of a public bank.

The discussion which ensued in the House, when, on February 27th, 1782, Mr. Eden (secretary to the Earl of Carlisle, then Lord Lieutenant) presented the heads of a Bill for establishing the Bank, forms an interesting comment on the popular notions of banking at that period. Mr. Eden delivered an elaborate address, commencing by stating that Ireland stood singular among commercial nations in the want of a public bank. He discussed the constitutions of the various banks, and said that it was proposed to adapt the projected institution after the model of the Bank of England. He urged that the lowering of interest as proposed by the Bill, might inspire a disposition to throw money into commerce, and by increasing industry, would promote frugality. Accumulation furnished the means of further loans at low interest; and thus the lowering of the rate tended to further reduce it. Mr. Ogle, who followed in the debate, considered that the scheme led to nothing but confusion and distress, and said he would never agree to any measure calculated to overturn public credit, and the commerce of the country. By such an experiment, Scotland was nearly ruined. It would be a most unjust and ungrateful return to the bankers of the country. In conclusion, he said "In justice, therefore, to those gentlemen, and to my country, I rise to oppose a lottery which may draw ruin upon our commerce." Sir Lucius O'Brien took a more enlightened view of the situation, and considered that there was not a person in the State from the most affluent subscriber to the lowest mechanic who would not be benefited by the Bank. Manufacturers would be able to obtain advances at five per cent., while at present they, sometimes, could not obtain money at any price whatever. Mr. Foster and Mr. Clements continued the debate in very much the same strain. Mr. Flood could not pretend to give a decided opinion on the subject for, though he had carefully read the best authors on banking, yet he did not find that any two of them agreed. The Bank of England had been near bankruptcy more than once. He, also, considered that it would be unjust to injure the private bankers. There was no analogy between England at the time the Bank of England was founded, and Ireland in 1782. The commerce of Ireland was comparatively nothing, but their circulation was the best in the world. Certain failures, no doubt, had happened, but the consequences of these failures had been the most perfect code of bankrupt laws ever contrived. The whole property of every banker was a stake to the public. Bankruptcies will happen in every trading country. The Bank of England had stopped payment, and had descended to the petty expedient of paying its notes in the smallest denomination of silver. It was proposed to give a certain number of men the power of converting paper into money, while the probability was the present bankers had already issued as much paper as the country could bear. The bank would foster speculation, and many abuses might arise within the institution, the import trade of the country would be unduly expanded, and manufacturers would be overwhelmed with a load of importations. The Provost of Dublin urged on the other hand, that the existing banks were on a scale infinitely below the demands of commerce, and complained that they were unable to give merchants the assistance they required. Sir John Blaquière attributed the opposition to the Bill, to the circumstance that it emanated from the Secretary of the Lord Lieutenant. It was not a splendid but a useful measure, and should be joyfully accepted by every friend to Ireland. Captain Burgh also concurred in this sentiment. He admitted that some merchants had petitioned against the Bill, but on what grounds? Were they so nervous that they could not bear the sudden joy of being told that they could in future discount their bills at five instead of six per cent.? The scheme had three great features, viz.:—permanency, low interest, and high security.

On March 5, a petition from several merchants and traders "praying time to consider of the scheme," having been presented, Mr. Eden gave notice of his intention to move that subscriptions should not be received prior to the 1st August, and that even after that day, the time of carrying the measure into execution, would depend on the circumstances of the country and the general disposition of the subscribers. He also gave notice of a motion that the proposed capital should be £600,000. The House then resolved itself into a Committee on the Bill, Mr. Mason being in the chair, when Mr. David La Touche and Sir Nicholas Lawless spoke in favour of the measure. Thereupon Mr. Bagenal moved the adjournment of the further consideration of the Bill, which, he complained, was being hurried through the House. He could not help expressing his surprise at the assertion that "lowering the interest of money tended still to lowering it more." If that were true we might hope to see the day when we should have money at nothing per cent. It was not high interest that prevented men embarking in trade, but it was "the usurped claim of the English Legislature supported now by a perpetual standing army." It was ridiculous for them to model themselves on the scale of old England—New England should be their model. Because England had an Exchange, must they have an awkward building? They were to have a bank because England had one, and perhaps three hundred millions debt, but the fable of the frog and the ox should be remembered. It had been observed that Ireland stood singular among commercial nations, but it was not so singular for want of a bank as for want of civil and commercial liberty. The motion for adjournment was, however, lost by 71, in a House of 115 members, and the Committee went through the Bill and agreed to their Report.

Under the Act 21 and 22 Geo. III., cap. 16, power was given to raise a capital of £600,000, Irish, of which no person was to subscribe more than £10,000, to be lent to Government at 4 per cent. The charter* was liable to withdrawal, after Jan. 1, 1794, on twelve months' previous notice, and repayment of all sums due by the Government. It was provided that the bank should not borrow more than the amount of its capital, nor pay nor charge more than 5 per cent. for loans or discounts, under a penalty of treble the sum lent.† It was also prohibited from lending money on mortgage, or dealing in any goods or merchandise, or from purchasing lands or revenues of the Crown,‡ or lending money to Government, except when authorised by Parliament. On the other hand, the virtual monopoly of the banking business of the country was secured to it under Section 14 of the Act, which provided that no other persons, exceeding six in number, should take up or owe any sums on their bills, etc., payable on demand, or for a less time than three months. This latter provision was foremost in importance, considered in relation to its results on the development of Irish commerce. In the light of later events, the toleration of so burdensome a monopoly, for a period of forty years, is almost inexplicable, and its subsequent removal marks a period in the commercial prosperity of the country, from which all after progress can be plainly traced.

---

* The charter was dated May 15, 1783.

† The legal rate of interest was then 6 per cent. (5 Geo. II., c. 7), and persons taking more were to lose treble the money lent, which was to be divided between the King and the informer. The rate was fixed in 1634 at 10 per cent., in 1704 it was reduced to 8 per cent., in 1721 to 7 per cent., and in 1731 to 6 per cent. Sir Henry Cavendish gave notice of his intention, in 1784, to introduce a Bill for lowering the rate to 5 per cent., but after some discussion in the House the matter was dropped. A similar measure was introduced in 1788.

‡ The private bankers had been in the habit of investing their surplus funds in land, as the only available investment, and the unrealisability of the security, in time of panic, was the cause of several failures.

The first Board of Directors was thus constituted :—

GOVERNOR : David La Touche, jun.

DEPUTY-GOVERNOR : Theophilus Thompson.

DIRECTORS :

John Allen.	**Sir Nicholas Lawless, Bart.**
Alexander Armstrong.	**George Palmer.**
William Colville.	**John La Touche.**
Samuel Dick.	**Peter La Touche.**
Jeremiah D'Olier.	**Amos Stettell.**
Travers Hartley.	**Jeremiah Vickers.**
George Godfrey Hoffman.	**Abraham Wilkinson.**
Alexander Jaffray.	

Mr. David La Touche, jun., was able to inform the House of Commons, on Oct. 31, 1783, that since the bank opened great advantage had been reaped therefrom, particularly by the traders in linen who had been advanced large sums at the rate of five per cent. per annum, and that the business was conducted in the most clear and regular manner. The balance of public money in the bank on October 27th in the same year was stated as £133,000.

At the time of its establishment, the directors were required to be Protestants, and to subscribe a declaration pursuant to an Act of Parliament entitled "an Act to prevent the further growth of Popery," but this provision was subsequently relaxed and afterwards removed.* Sir Robert Peel, on the introduction of the Irish Banking Bill in the House of Commons, on April 25th, 1845, said "I am bound also to say, that the Bank of Ireland, consisting for the most part of persons professing the Protestant religion, were the first to ask that certain oaths, distinguishing their Roman Catholic brethren from themselves should be altogether abolished. It is their earnest wish that no oath should be administered as a necessary qualification for becoming a director of the Bank of Ireland, except the simple oath of allegiance, and the oath as to the amount of property which it is necessary to possess in order to qualify for the office. They state—these respectable gentlemen who are connected with the Bank of Ireland—that it is painful to their feelings, that when a Roman Catholic director of that

* 8 and 9 Victoria, cap. 37.

bank is appointed, he is sent into a separate room, in order that a separate oath may be administered to him, and it is at their express instance that I ask, that, for the future, there should be no distinction between the oaths administered to Protestant and Roman Catholic directors of the Bank of Ireland."

The bank commenced business in June, 1783, in some old houses in Mary's Abbey, Dublin. In 1802, after the Union of Great Britain and Ireland, the directors purchased the Parliament House for £40,000 (Irish), and having adapted it to their requirements, removed there in 1808. The original cost of the edifice, which was completed in 1739, was £40,000, and, in addition, a sum of £30,000 had been expended on the Western front in 1783. The meetings of the directors and shareholders are held in the chamber which once constituted the meeting place of the Lords, while the Commons' House is converted into the general office.

The Charter was renewed in 1791 by the 31 Geo. III., c. 22, increasing the capital of the bank to £1,000,000. In 1797, by the 37 Geo. III., c. 50, a further £500,000 was added, and in 1808, by the 48 Geo. III., c. 103, the charter was again extended until the expiration of twelve months' notice, to be given after January 1st, 1837, and the capital increased by £1,000,000, making £2,500,000. The last increase of capital was in 1820, by 1 and 2 George IV., c. 72, when £500,000 was added, making together £3,000,000 Irish,* under circumstances which will be referred to later on. On the establishment of the bank, instructions were given to the various government departments to pay to it all receipts from revenue, and the teller of the Exchequer was directed to draw on the bank against such receipts.†

The frontispiece of this work consists of a fac-simile of one of the earliest issued Bank of Ireland notes. It bears date of March 4th, 1808. The author is indebted to the authorities of the bank for the loan of the original note, and the permission to re-produce it.

From the period of its establishment until the year 1797, no incident in the history of the bank calls for special observation. The bank seems, meanwhile, to have pursued the even tenor of its way.

---

* Equal to £2,769,230 15*s*. 5*d*. sterling money of Great Britain.

† 25 Geo. III., c. 28, s. 17.

Although its operations were confined to the capital, its existence apparently acted as a salutary check on the number of private banks in all parts of the country. In the whole of Ireland there were only nine private banks, of which three were in Dublin, and this number cannot be considered excessive in view of the large increase in the population—amounting to some sixty or seventy per cent.—during the interval between 1783 and 1797.

In the latter year, on the suspension of cash payments by the Bank of England, a similar concession was accorded "for the sake of uniformity," to the Bank of Ireland. Whatever may have been the necessity for the suspension of cash payments in England, there was no adequate reason for the extension of the concession to Ireland, nor was it preceded by any enquiry into the state of the kingdom. The exchange was at that time, and had been for a long time previously, regularly in its favour; no apprehension of a drain of gold existed; and there had been no sufficient demand on the bank to justify the measure.

The natural effect of the suspension of cash payments was a great increase in the note circulation. In 1797 the circulation amounted to only £621,917; in 1825 the figures had swelled to £6,309,300, as will be seen in the following table:—

Bank of Ireland.—Average Note Circulation 1797–1802, and 1808–1825.

Year.	Circulation.	Year.	Circulation.	Year.	Circulation.
	£		£		£
1797	621 917	1810	3.157,300	1818	4,432,400
1798	737.268	1811	3,501,000	1819	4.297,000
1799	1,737,879	1812	3,791,100	1820	4,241,700
1800	2,482,162	1813	4,212,600	1821	5.182,600
1801	2,626,471	1814	4,418,900	1822	5.122,800
1802	2,816,669	1815	4,304,000	1823	5,070,500
1808	2,827,000	1816	4,191,000	1824	5,579,700
1809	3,068,100	1817	4.390,800	1825	6,309.300

These were also red-letter days for the bank proprietors. The dividends distributed from 1783 to 1836 were as follows :—

		£			£			£
1783–4	...	5	*1797	...	19	*1806–7	...	10
1785	...	5¾	1798–9	...	6½	1808	...	7½
1786–90	...	6	1800	...	7	*1809–14	...	10
1791	...	5½	1801	...	7¼	1815–20	...	10
1792	...	5⅜	1802	...	7½	*1821	...	30
1793	...	5¼	*1803	...	12½	1822–9	...	10
1794	...	5½	1804	...	7½	1830–5	...	9
1795	...	6	*1805	...	12½	1836	...	8½
1796	...	6½						

Again, in 1797, the exchange on London was 5½ to 6¾ (the par. being 8⅓). In 1801, it had risen to 11¾–13, and in 1804 was as high as 18. The price of bullion and guineas also rose to 10 per cent. above the Mint price.

Reference has already been made to the over-issues of the private banks during the same period, to the large increase in their number after 1797, and to their almost entire extinction between that year and 1820. The result was that, with the exception of the cities of Dublin, Cork and Belfast, the country was without any banking accommodation whatever.

In this situation of affairs, the government of Lord Liverpool at length turned their attention to the matter, with a view to the institution of a more secure system of banking, in harmony with the needs of the people. The Act 1 and 2 Geo. IV., c. 72, was passed in 1820, and under it the Bank of Ireland was permitted to increase its capital to £3,000,000 (Irish), in return for which concession it parted with so much of its monopoly as enabled banking companies with more than six partners to carry on business at a distance of fifty (Irish) miles† from Dublin, and to borrow, owe, or take up, any sum or sums of money on their notes or bills payable on demand. But the Act according this privilege was destined to remain in abeyance for more than four years. It was successfully maintained that every partner in a

* Including Bonus.

† Equal to sixty-five English miles.

joint stock bank must be resident in Ireland, a provision never contemplated by the framers of the Act, and the exclusion of English capitalists thus greatly restricted the formation of any new bank. For four years, therefore, the Act remained a dead letter. Amending Acts were passed in 1824–1825* to remedy this difficulty, enabling persons resident in any part of Great Britain or Ireland to become shareholders.

In 1828, the Act 9 George IV., cap. 80, placed the Irish banks on the same footing as those in England, enabling them to issue unstamped notes upon payment of a composition, in lieu of the stamp duties thereon, on the actual amount of notes in circulation. In 1842† the assimilation of the Irish stamp duties to those of Great Britain more than doubled the existing impost.

The radius of fifty Irish miles round Dublin was still sacred to the Bank of Ireland, under the Act of 1820, and until 1845 no bank consisting of more than six partners could carry on its operations within that charmed circle. The Provincial Bank, which had in the meantime been established, found it necessary, for the convenience of their customers, and to facilitate the conduct of their business, to open an office in the capital, where they also paid their notes, but did not re-issue them. The law apparently permitted the establishment of these houses of business for the purpose of agency, but not for the keeping of accounts or the issue or payment of notes. The Bank of Ireland, guarding the monopoly remaining to them with, perhaps, pardonable jealousy, saw, in the payment of the Provincial Bank's notes in Dublin, an infringement of their charter, and in December, 1828, they instituted an action against them on that ground. The jury found, as they were bound to do on the evidence, a verdict for the plaintiffs, but, in assessing the damages at sixpence and awarding a like amount for costs, they indicated their sense of the injustice of the restriction. The verdict of the jury reflected the feeling of the merchants of Dublin at that time. The monopoly of the Bank of Ireland placed them at a disadvantage compared with traders in other towns where the banking accommodation was better and less exclusive.

* 5 George IV., c. 73 (1824) repealed, with certain exceptions, by 6 George IV., c. 42 (1825).

† 5 and 6 Vict., cap. 82.

They had already petitioned the Lords of the Treasury on the expediency of entering into a new agreement with the Bank of Ireland to permit the establishment of joint stock banks in the city of Dublin, but their request had been unheeded.* The result of this action, however, led to a compromise between the two banks, and an Act of Parliament, 1 William IV., c. 32, was passed in 1830, legalising the payment of notes in Dublin for the purpose only of withdrawing them from circulation at the option of the bank issuing them. It was also arranged that the Provincial Bank should make a confidential return to the Chancellor of the Exchequer for the time being of the amount of notes issued or current from time to time in every year.

With this exception, the Bank of Ireland retained the privileges granted to it by the Act 1 and 2 Geo. IV., until 1845, when by the Act 8 and 9 Victoria, cap. 37, the whole country was thrown open to banking enterprise. The main provisions of this latter Act are commented upon in Chapter XI., and the full text of the measure is given in the Appendix.

Until 1886 the bank did not issue any balance-sheet to the public, and its statistical history, glimpses of which are occasionally to be seen in Parliamentary Reports, is therefore of an irregular and desultory kind. The following figures show the position on December 31st, 1888 :—

Liabilities to Stockholders	£2,769,231
Liabilities to the Public	12,239,706
Rest	1,034,000
Net profits for half year	152,453
Dividend per cent per annum. . . .	11
Assets	16,201,039

* Memorial of the merchants, traders and others, of Dublin, to the Lords of the Treasury, 1826.

CHAPTER VI.

THE PROVINCIAL BANK OF IRELAND.

Projection in 1824—Establishment in 1825—Capital—Selection of London for the Head Office—Branches—Directors—Competition and opposition of the Bank of Ireland—Privileges accorded to it—Panics encountered—Anecdotes of the panics—Net Profits, Dividend and Reserve 1827–1888—Extracts from the Reports—The Provincial Bank was the real pioneer of Irish banking.

AFTER the numerous failures of the private banks culminating in the disasters of 1820, referred to in a previous chapter, there were, outside Dublin, only two towns in the kingdom possessing banks, viz.: Cork and Belfast, though two very small concerns still survived in Mallow and Wexford. The Bank of Ireland had no establishment outside Dublin. It will thus be seen that a very extensive field for banking operations existed, when the monopoly of the Bank of Ireland was partially swept away by the Legislature.

Influenced by these considerations, a number of gentlemen held a meeting in London on June 11th, 1824, and it was then resolved to form a bank, to be styled the Provincial Bank of Ireland, with a capital of £2,000,000, in 20,000 shares of £100 each, of which £500,000, or £25 per share, was to be paid up. The scheme was at first looked upon as Utopian, but towards the end of the year applications were received for an amount far exceeding the sum required. It is to be remarked that the only addition to the paid-up capital of the Bank since its foundation has been a sum of £40,000 taken from the Rest in 1836, and making the present total of £540,000.

The prohibitive clauses in the Act of 1820, compelling the residence in Ireland of every partner in a joint stock bank, delayed the commencement of business until the Amending Act (6 Geo. IV., c. 42) was passed in 1825, and it was not until 1st September in the latter year, that the first branch was opened at Cork. The Deed of Settlement bearing date of 1st August, 1825, was signed by 692 shareholders. Messrs. La Touche and Co. were appointed agents in Dublin, and acted in that capacity until 1st January, 1838, when the Bank opened its own office at No. 60, William Street. This agency was converted into a branch in December, 1845, after the passing of the Act 8 and 9 Victoria, cap. 37.

The head office of the bank was located in London, a selection necessitated by the fact that the Bank of Ireland monopoly would have prohibited the opening of a Dublin Office. It is probable, however, that much of the success of the bank has been due to this arrangement. Apart from the opportunities London affords of securing a high-class directorate, and of its position as a monetary centre, the advantages of a board of management at a distance from the field of operations and free from local prejudices and interests, have been abundantly manifested. Local Directors with limited powers were, however, at first appointed at each branch.

The following is a list of the Branches in the order of their establishment :—

Cork	1825	Cavan	1834
Limerick	„	Omagh	„
Clonmel	„	Dungannon	„
Londonderry	„	Bandon	„
Sligo	1826	Ennis	1835
Wexford	„	Ballyshannon	„
Belfast	„	Strabane	„
Waterford	„	Dungarvan	1835
Galway	„	Mallow	„
Armagh	1827	Cootehill	1837
Athlone	„	Kilrush	1838
Coleraine	„	Skibbereen	1839
Kilkenny	„	Enniscorthy	1841
Ballina	1828	Fermoy	1843
Tralee	„	Dublin	1845
Youghal	1831	Newry	1846
Enniskillen	„	Drogheda	„
Monaghan	1832	Nenagh	1856
Banbridge	1833	Templemore	„
Ballymena	„	Carrick-on-Suir	„
Parsonstown	„	Carrick-on-Shannon	1858

Clogheen	1860	Bantry	1886
Newcastle, Co. Limerick .	1861	Kinsale	1887
Kanturk	1877		
Tipperary . . .	1878	SUB-BRANCHES.	
Listowel	1879	Bundoran	1886
Capel Street, Dublin. .	1882	Killaloe	,,
Swinford	1884	Warren Point . . .	1887

In addition, the following branches have been opened, and closed when found unsuccessful :—

	Opened.	Closed.		Opened.	Closed.
Downpatrick .	1834	1848	Carlow . .	1846	1846
Lurgan . .	,,	1847	Macroom . .	1885	1885
Moneymore .	1835	1843	Kilmallock . .	1885	1885
Dundalk . .	1846	1849			

Sub-branches were opened in 1885 at Newmarket, Fethard, Dunmanway, Bruff, and Kinfanane, and closed in the same year.

The first Board of Directors was thus constituted :—

Matthias Attwood, M.P. (partner in Spooner, Attwood and Co.,* the London Bankers of the Provincial Bank).
Edward Blount.
George Robert Dawson, M.P. (brother-in-law to Sir Robert Peel).
Henry Alexander Douglas.
Oliver Farrer.
Sir Robert Townsend Farquhar, Bart., M.P.
Edward Fletcher.
Thomas Potter Macqueen.
Samuel Eustace Mangan.
William Medley.
Moses Montefiore (afterwards Sir Moses Montefiore).
Charles Elton Prescott.
Thomas Spring Rice, M.P. (afterwards Lord Monteagle).
John Thomas Thorp, Alderman.
Samuel Nevil Ward.
John Wright.

As has been stated, the operations of the Bank of Ireland had hitherto been confined to Dublin. Alive, suddenly, to the necessity of competition with rivals which were becoming formidable, they reversed this principle, and opening branches in the principal towns pursued a

* Amalgamated with Messrs. Barclay, Bevan and Co. in 1863.

vigorous policy of retaliation. On the publication of the Provincial Bank's prospectus announcing the names of towns in which branches would be established, the Bank of Ireland opened an office at Cork, and immediately afterwards established branches at Waterford, Clonmel, Londonderry, Newry, Belfast and Westport. The field of the new bank's operations was thus considerably narrowed.

In addition, the vested rights of the Bank of Ireland presented a formidable difficulty. In 1830, as the result of the litigation between the two banks referred to in the preceding chapter, the Act 1 William IV., cap. 32, was passed, legalising the payment of notes in Dublin for the purpose, only, of withdrawing them from circulation. But, notwithstanding this concession, the remaining privileges of the Bank of Ireland operated very disadvantageously to the Provincial Bank, and, owing to the ambiguity of the law, doubtful questions were constantly recurring. One point of difficulty which may be mentioned was the exact extent of the fifty-mile radius. In the case of Newry, the fiftieth mile-stone was in the middle of the town, and the bank considered that they had a right to establish their branch beyond that mile-stone. Subsequently the road was shortened, and the question arose whether they were acting illegally in establishing a branch beyond fifty miles by the old road, and less than fifty miles by the new one.* The importance of the point lay in the fact that by committing a legal mistake in one of their acts, they would lose the benefit of the Acts under which they were formed, the whole of their transactions would become illegal, and they would be liable to penalties for the whole amount of their issues.†

In 1827 the privilege was accorded to the Provincial Bank of receiving the revenue of the Irish Excise, Stamps and Post Office receipts beyond the Dublin district reserved to the Bank of Ireland. A Treasury Order in the same year authorised Collectors of Revenue

---

* It is to be remarked that the circle of fifty miles is not a complete one as Dublin stands on the coast. The privileged radius was, therefore, only semi-circular.

† Evidence of Mr. Peirce Mahony before the House of Commons' Committee, 1837.

to receive the notes of the bank in payment of revenue, in the same manner as those of the Bank of Ireland.

It will be seen from the figures given below that the progress of the institution realised every expectation, but in addition to the rivalry of the Bank of Ireland, and the ignorance of banking methods among the people, many difficulties had to be encountered. During the first few years of its existence successive runs for gold had to be met, at a cost, which having regard to the expense and risk attending the movement of specie must have been considerable. The first run took place so early in its history as February and March, 1826, in Cork, owing to the unexpected discontinuance of two local banks through the death of one and the failure of the other banker. It unfortunately happened that the demand for gold could only be met by the Provincial Bank, the Bank of Ireland not being then liable to pay in gold except in Dublin.

Again in October, 1828, in June and July, 1830, and in January, 1831, runs, mainly in the South of Ireland, had to be contended, the results of panic arising out of circumstances of political excitement. In the two latter cases the Bank of Ireland shared, with the Provincial Bank, the brunt of supplying gold in the provinces, as the Act 9 Geo. IV., c. 81, had meanwhile been passed, placing the Bank of Ireland on an equality with the other banks as regards making all notes payable at the places where issued.

Another run, this time equally directed against the Bank of Ireland and the Savings Banks, and again excited by political agitation, commenced in the south of Ireland in February and March, 1833.

In November, 1836, on the failure of the Agricultural Bank, there was a general run on all the Irish Banks, which was intensified by a scarcity of money in London, so extreme that even Exchequer Bills were all but inconvertible. In preparation for it the Provincial Bank had on hand a sum in gold, exceeding the amount of their issue. Mr. Peirce Mahony in his evidence before the House of Commons Committee in 1837, stated that the supply of gold taken from the Bank of England, for Ireland, during this panic, which lasted about a month, did not fall far short of £2,000,000. In February, 1839, a run on another bank took place in Cork, but the demands on the Provincial Bank were inconsiderable.

This record of panic appears to have ceased, so far as the Provincial Bank is concerned, in November, 1856, when the stoppage of the Royal British Bank, the Tipperary Joint Stock Bank, and some English country institutions, caused a run on all the banks which, however, being promptly met, soon subsided.

During this latter panic, a farmer is reported to have entered one of the branches of the bank to demand repayment of some five hundred pounds, the hard savings of years, and having been waiting since cock-crow to be the first in, he was surprised to find the teller unconcernedly paying away the precious coin. He received the amount of his deposit, and in addition, the official handed him the interest due to him. "What's this for?" said the honest man. "For your interest," the clerk replied. "'Tis surely for my interest," was the rejoinder, "but are you not giving me what belongs to them that wants it themselves?" "Take your interest, my good man," the clerk said, "it has been lying here for you this long time." "Oh! murther!" ejaculated the simple man "and that's what Councillor Deasy was at, asking for my vote and interest; I gave him my vote with a heart-and-a-half, but 'twas the will of heaven I was besaid by the Misthus to run on the bank to be beforehand with him, or I never would have seen a sight of my interest." Another anecdote of the same period, though unconnected with the Provincial Bank, may be here recorded. In this case, a tenant whose arrears of rent had been hopelessly longed for, presented himself smilingly to his landlord, thumbed down his notes and got his receipt. The servant, letting him out, declared that it was a "sign before death" to see him paying his rent. "It is," said Mike, with a grin, "there's my receipt, and the bank's broke, and the best thing you can do is to advise the master to give what he got to a charity, before 'tis found out." *

The Provincial Bank is one of the oldest joint stock banks in the United Kingdom. During its career it has enjoyed great prosperity, the first interruption being in 1875, when, owing to disastrous failures in Belfast and the North of Ireland, losses, estimated at £75,000, were experienced, which were provided for, to the extent of £37,200, by a fund set aside in former years to meet exceptional bad debts.

---

* Bankers' Magazine, Vol. XVII.

The following statement shows the progress of the bank :—

Year.	Net Profits.	Dividend and Bonus.	Rest.	No. of Brnchs.	Year.	Net Profits.	Dividend and Bonus.	Rest.	No. of Brnchs.
	£	%	£			£	%	£	
1827	28,700	4	14,700	11	1858	116,469	20	234,384	41
8	22,200	4	16,900	15	9	110,138	20	236,521	42
9	22,600	4	19,500	15	1860	111,783	20	240,305	42
1830	21,800	4	21,364	15	1	119,389	20	251,693	44
1	21,800	5	23,164	15	2	111,356	20	255,048	44
2	34,068	5	32,228	18	3	103,864	20	250,913	44
3	42,971	6	50,199	20	4	109,954	20	252,868	44
4	56,317	7	76,516	21	5	111,696	20	256,563	44
5	61,049	8	102,565	30	6	104,396	20	252,959	44
6	61,791	8	124,355	33	7	110,059	20	255,018	44
7	45,943	8	88,699	34	8	101,699	20	248,717	44
8	47,375	8	92,874	34	9	108,189	20	248,906	44
9	56.774	10	106,448	36	1870	103,024	20	243,930	44
1840	59,531	8	101,178	36	1	104,421	20	240,352	44
1	47.514	8	105,492	37	2	113.205	20	245,557	44
2	51.908	10	114,200	37	3	111.544	20	249,101	44
3	49.402	8	97,121	37	4	113,030	20	254.131	44
4	47,413	8	99,423	36	5	99,524	18	213,255	44
5	49,721	8	104,134	37	6	97,200	15	197,319	44
6	53,989	8	114,924	42	7	82,129	15	198,448	44
7	54,473	10	126,197	40	8	85,521	15	202.969	45
8	46,109	8	107,506	40	9	89,618	15	211,587	46
9	45,733	8	110,039	39	1880	71,230	13	201,817	47
1850	43,344	8	110,182	38	1	67,647	13	199,264	47
1	45,395	8	112,378	38	2	57,319	10	186,383	47
2	47,659	8	116.837	38	3	78,307	12	174,000	48
3	58,511	10	132,148	38	4	68,305	12	174,000	49
4	77,970	10	145,318	38	5	61,553	11	174,000	51
5	81,698	10	162,217	38	6	57,056	10	174,000	51
6	99,371	10	196,788	40	7	54.035	10	174,000	51
7	115,537	20	225.915	41	8	56.786	10	174,000	51

Although the Annual Reports do not disclose any figures other than those relating to profits, until the adoption of limited liability in 1882, they leave nothing to be desired as regards information on the state of the country and the progress of the Bank's business. In fact, they may be said to form in themselves an epitome of Irish history, and include a large amount of detail in regard to social and political questions. In the days when railways were not so general as they are now, it was necessary to place full information before shareholders at a distance.

The following extract, while serving to indicate the wide scope of these Reports, is also of some antiquarian interest. It refers to the commercial failures of 1839–40 :—

"The number has been increased by a cause which certainly presents a novelty in the history of Ireland, namely, the progress of temperance, which has been so surprisingly promoted in the South and partly in the West of Ireland, and of which the effect has been to paralyse to a great degree the business of distillers and brewers, and to put an end to the trade of many who gained their living as publicans by the sale of spirituous or fermented liquors. That much good to the people and to the country will result from this movement is not to be doubted, but it is not the less true that to the classes just mentioned it is productive of much present distress, and as regards bankers, that it operates injuriously against the regular payment of bills."

In a following report it is stated that :—

"The prevalence of temperance has been so extensive and sudden, as nearly to annihilate the business of numerous distillers and brewers, not to mention publicans."

The Provincial Bank was the real pioneer of Irish banking. It fell to the lot of that institution to combat with existing prejudices, to guide legislation, and step by step to secure freedom of trade in banking. In such a work as this, its history is, therefore, deserving of extended notice.

CHAPTER VII.

THE IRISH JOINT STOCK BANKS.

Northern Bank—Capital and Dividends—Hibernian Bank—Efforts to obtain powers of issue—Circulation of tokens—Business—Reserve Fund—Changes in Capital—Reconstitution—Present position—Belfast Bank—Capital, dividends and liabilities—National Bank—System on which it was established—Consolidation of the capital—Opening of a London office—Objection raised by the Bank of England—The connection of Mr. Daniel O'Connell with the National Bank—Conflict between Inspectors and Directors in 1850—The Liberator's plate and testimonials—Progress of business—Royal Bank of Ireland—Intended connection with the Agricultural Bank—Efforts to obtain power of issue—Election of Directors—Bank premises—Business in 1847—Progress of business 1837-1888—Ulster Bank—Capital, reserve, dividends, and liabilities, 1837-1888—Munster and Leinster Bank—Analysis of balance sheets.

THE remaining seven joint stock banks are dealt with in the order of their establishment.

The first joint stock bank to take advantage of the Act of 1824 was the Northern Banking Company, founded on a private bank* of the same name in Belfast, which commenced business in January, 1825, with a nominal capital of £500,000. An attempt had been made to start the bank in 1820 in conformity with the law as it then stood, but this had not been found practicable. In 1867, the Company was incorporated, and the subscribed capital increased to £1,000,000. It has since been further increased to £2,000,000, with £400,000 paid up. The bank adopted limited liability on September 1st, 1883. The dividends paid during the last six half-years, have been at the rate of 11 per cent. on the A. shares, and 5½ per cent. on the B. shares. In 1888, the Northern Bank purchased, at a cost of £22,500,

* The partners were Messrs. Orr, McCance, McNeile and Montgomery.

the business of Messrs. Ball and Company, of Dublin, and in the same year opened an office in the capital.

The Hibernian Bank, originally styled the "Hibernian Joint Stock Loan and Annuity Company" was established under a special Act of Parliament (5 Geo. IV., c. 159) with a subscribed capital of £1,000,000, and commenced business in June, 1825. The bank was promoted by the Roman Catholics, who were at that time excluded from the direction of the Bank of Ireland. Endeavours were also made to obtain the power of issuing notes, but on the opposition of the Bank of Ireland the clauses were expunged in committee. On the failure of this attempt, an effort was made to reap the advantages of a bank of issue by the circulation of tokens, which were issued on engraved unstamped paper, and thus expressed, "Hibernian Bank Token, One Pound," with signature and date. It was contended, and the law was construed to hold, that these tokens were not notes, but the opposition of the Bank of Ireland led to their subsequent withdrawal. This excited considerable discontent among a portion of the shareholders, and a Bill for the dissolution of the company was introduced into the House of Commons but was rejected. A renewed, but again unsuccessful, effort to obtain the privilege of issuing notes was made in 1844.

In its early days the bank enjoyed considerable prosperity, and distributed good dividends, but its operations during the last few years have been, so far as the proprietors are concerned, of a less satisfactory character. In 1878, and again in 1881, incursions had to be made into the reserve fund, which was at length entirely wiped out, and the dividends fell to zero. The pruning knife seems to have been very vigorously applied and the bank has since made fair headway.

The value and utility of a substantial reserve to meet unforeseen contingencies, has thus been proved in the case of the Hibernian Bank, though, in 1847, some of the shareholders looked with jealousy on the growth of the fund. At the meeting in that year, notice of a motion was given that "the proprietors ought to receive ordinary interest on the profits of the Company as well as on their shares of the paid up capital, regard being had to the reserve fund contemplated by the original deed of settlement."

The original capital of £1,000,000, with £250,000 paid up, was increased in 1868 to £1,500,000, with £375,000 paid up, and in 1873 to £2,000,000, with £500,000 paid up, at which figure it now stands. The nominal amount of each share was £100, with £25 paid up, until 1885, when the company was reconstituted, the name was changed to "The Hibernian Bank, Limited," and the capital subdivided into shares of £20, with £5 paid up.

The following extracts from the balance sheet at December 31st, 1888, shew the present position of the bank :—

LIABILITIES.		ASSETS.	
To Shareholders . .	£500,000	Cash	£136,671
To the Public . . .	1,350,526	Investments . . .	174,681
		Loans and Discounts including money at call .	1,456,244
		Bank Premises, Head Office and 32 branches .	110,692
	£1,850,526		£1,878,288

There is a provision fund for doubtful debts, but the amount is not stated, and it may be remarked that the liability of the shareholders largely exceeds the total liability of the bank to the public.

The Belfast Banking Company, originally a private institution carrying on business under the same style, commenced business on August 1st, 1827, with a nominal capital of £500,000, of which £125,000 was paid up. The bank was registered as a company with limited liability, on August 16th, 1883. The following figures shew the progress of the business, but the information is necessarily limited, as no balance sheets were published prior to 1882 :—

—	Capital Subscribed.	Paid-up.
	£	£
1827 to 1865	500,000	125,000
1866 — 1882	1,000,000	250,000
Since 1883	2,000,000	400,000

Year.	Reserve Fund.	Year.	Liabilities to the Public.
	£		£
1874	185,966	1882	2,894,794
1879	205,137	1885	2,650,710
1883	227,227	1888	2,923,699
1888	349,272*	—	—

Since 1874, dividends have been annually paid of 20 per cent. on the old shares and 8 per cent. on the new capital.

In 1835, one year after the establishment of the Agricultural Bank, the National Bank of Ireland,† promoted by the Nationalist party, commenced business at Carrick-on-Suir with a subscribed capital of £1,000,000. The bank was founded on a curious system. At first it consisted of two distinct bodies—the English and Irish shareholders. When a branch was opened the local shareholders subscribed a proportion of the capital and the English proprietors contributed a like amount, the profits being equally divided between them. In the year 1837, to remove inconveniences found to arise from this arrangement, the two stocks were consolidated throughout the branches except two, viz., Clonmel with a paid-up capital of £16,235, and Carrick-on-Suir with a paid-up capital of £4,962 10*s*. where the local shareholders finding their opportunities unusually profitable, were unwilling to share them with the whole proprietary. In 1856, however, the consolidation of the business was effected, and these two branches relinquished their separate existence.

Mr. Gilbart, in his work on "The Principles and Practice of Banking" says that this principle was first introduced to the public by the late Mr. Thomas Joplin. He attempted to introduce it into the National Provincial Bank of England, of which he was the managing director, and to the formation of which he had materially

* Including £60,000 added to the Reserve Fund, for premium on 6,000 new shares.

† The title was changed to the National Bank in 1856, after the transaction of London banking business was commenced.

contributed. But the practical difficulties were found to be great. It was almost impossible to arrange the preliminaries to the satisfaction of all parties, and the principle was never brought into operation. Mr. Lamie Murray, who projected the National Bank of Ireland, was the Secretary to the National Provincial Bank of England, and had adopted Mr. Joplin's views on the subject.

The bank having taken power, in its deed of settlement, to transact banking business in any part of the United Kingdom, commenced, in 1854, the transaction of banking business in London. The Bank of England objected to their doing so, under the Act 7 and 8 Victoria, c. 32, restricting the introduction of any issuing bank in London which had not been established previously to May 6th, 1844, in the terms of the Act. The opinions of Sir R. Bethell, afterwards Lord Westbury, Mr. Bovill, afterwards Lord Chief Justice Bovill, and other eminent counsel, were taken by both parties, and were in favour of the National Bank, it being held that at the time of its formation the bank had two objects in view, the one to become bankers in England the other in Ireland, and that, although it had suspended carrying into effect the former, and had only, up to that time, carried out the latter object, the company was, nevertheless, on May 6th, 1844, established within the meaning of the Act.

The personal fidelity of the Irish to their political leaders is exemplified in the early progress of the National Bank. The first Governor was Mr. Daniel O'Connell, and the young institution, becoming known as the "Liberator's Bank," extended its issue of notes with remarkable rapidity. But on Mr. O'Connell's death, in 1847, injurious reports were circulated to the effect that the late governor was indebted to the Bank to the extent of £60,000 or £70,000, and it was found necessary to make a public announcement that the amount due did not exceed £4,000, which was covered by Policies of Insurance for £7,500, and other securities.

In 1850–1851, the Bank suffered from internal troubles of, happily, an unusual character. Charges were brought by the three inspectors against the directors of gross inattention to the interests of the bank. It was alleged that they had abused the confidence reposed in them for their personal advantage, that they had taken loans for themselves on insufficient security or without security at all, that they had made use of the branch managers to obtain proxies to influence the election of directors and to remove obnoxious directors who had opposed such irregular proceedings from their seats at the Board, and that they had declared a dividend which had not been earned. The chairman, Mr. T. Lamie Murray, was also charged with having used his influence to promote the interests of an Assurance Company, the National Loan Fund Life Assurance Society, which was stated to be in an embarrassed condition. These charges were met by the directors by a resolution dismissing the Inspectors from the service of the bank, but the matter could not, of course, rest in this position, and the directors were applied to by some of the shareholders to call a special meeting for the consideration of the subject. The result of this meeting was that the Inspectors were re-instated, and that five of the directors, Mr. T. Lamie Murray, Mr. Nicolas Maher, M.P., Mr. Maurice O'Connell, M.P., Mr. Anthony O'Flaherty, M.P., and Mr. FitzSimon, a son-in-law of the Liberator, were required to resign. This resolution seems to have been founded solely on the ground that the five directors had borrowed money from the bank and were thus, without regard to the circumstances that in some cases the amount was small and amply secured, disqualified from sitting at the Board. In fact the total amount owing was only some £19,000, of which £13,000 was due by two out of the five directors. This incident, though no doubt at the time it was the cause of considerable unpleasantness, did not injuriously affect the interests of the bank. On the contrary, a deputation of the shareholders having been afforded an investigation into its affairs, arrived at the satisfactory conclusion that everything was sound and prosperous, and that no stain was attached to the conduct of any of the directors.

The Report for 1855 stated that "The decease of the late Mr. Maurice O'Connell obviously necessitated the closing of his account by disposing of the various collateral securities held by the bank, all of which, with one exception, have been realised, and the proceeds placed to his credit; that exception the directors hope the proprietors will consider an honourable one, being the plate of the late Mr. Daniel O'Connell, and mostly testimonials presented to him on different public occasions, which, on his death, had descended to his heir, Mr. Maurice O'Connell, and of which the Board felt confident, that it would never be the wish of the proprietors, under any circumstances, to deprive the family. They therefore took upon themselves to restore it to the present heir, Mr. Daniel O'Connell, eldest son of Mr. Maurice O'Connell, as a gift in the name of the proprietors and which the directors confidently rely will have their hearty concurrence."

The following figures show the progress of the business during the last twenty-five years :—

Year.	Paid-up Capital.	Reserve Fund.	Deposits.	Other Liabilities.	Dividend and Bonus.
	£	£	£	£	%
1863	600.000	143,729	4,208,156	1,115.458	13½
1868	1,500,000	175,900	5,047,431	1,601,111	8
1873	,,	123,000	8.124,625	1,347.956	10
1878	,,	145,000	8,097,794	1.309,347	12
1883	,,	218,689	9.302.628	1.423.102	11
1888	,,	241,889	9,238,730	1,490,248	9

It will thus be seen that the National Bank has flourished exceedingly, and in point of the magnitude of its business, it takes a high place among kindred institutions, not only in Ireland, but throughout the United Kingdom.

The Ulster Bank came into existence in 1836, with a head office at Belfast. The original capital was £1,000,000, which has since been increased to £2,400,000, with £400,000 paid up. In 1862 a branch was opened in Dublin. It will be seen from the following table that the bank has enjoyed the same prosperity as the two other banks of the province from which it takes its name :—

Ulster Bank, Limited.

Year ended 1st Sept.	Paid-up Capital.	Reserve Funds.	Dividend per annum.	Liabilities to the Public.	Year ended 1st Sept.	Paid-up Capital.	Reserve Funds.	Dividend per annum.	Liabilities to the Public.
	£	£	%	£		£	£	%	£
1837	204,600	...	5	160,477	1863	183,405	95,608	12	1,828,676
1838	204,875	...	6	299,490	1864	183,405	100,000	16	2,030,377
1839	204,875		6½	300,324	1865	183,405	103,000	18	2,491,229
1840	204,875	...	7	322,568	1866	183,405	110,000	20	2,770,118
1841	206,025	...	7	381,170	1867	183,405	115,000	20	2,855,974
1842	206,025	...	6½	380,391	1868	183,405	120,000	20	2,783,247
1843	206,025	...	5	401,416	1869	183,405	125,000	20	2,826,890
1844	193,385	...	5	474,095	1870	183,405	130,000	20	2,930,626
1845	193,285	...	5	626,573	1871	183,405	135,000	20	3,234,654
1846	191,785	...	5	640,839	1872	250,000	250,000	20	3,472,072
1847	191,622	...	5	546,925	1873	250,000	285,000	20	3,629,779
1848	190,710	...	5	527,396	1874	250,000	287,500	20	3,709,764
1849	186,187	...	5	547,302	1875	250,000	292,500	20	4,029,236
1850	183,630	...	5	649,512	1876	250,000	300,000	20	4,316,194
1851	183,530	...	5	767,985	1877	300,000	350,000	20	4,314,549
1852	183,530	...	5	855,592	1878	300,000	350,000	20	4,142,829
1853	183,530	...	5½	1,124,689	1879	300,000	350,000	20	3,791,456
1854	183,530	26,325	6	1,351,377	1880	300,000	350,000	20	3,814,044
1855	183,405	33,557	6½	1,303,995	1881	300,000	350,000	20	3,721,453
1856	183,405	46,223	7½	1,503,220	1882	300,000	350,000	20	4,161,469
1857	183,405	61,579	8½	1,686,892	1883	383,095	364,042	20	4,154,870
1858	183,405	66,266	9	1,577,613	1884	400,000	418,126	20	4,077,127
1859	183,405	67,644	9	1,761,719	1885	400,000	450,000	20	4,032,155
1860	183,405	71,550	9½	1,853,267	1886	400,000	450,000	18	4,177,714
1861	183,405	83,570	10	1,900,789	1887	400,000	450,000	18	4,277,173
1862	183,405	88,475	10	1,922,430	1888	400,000	450.000	18	4,513,086

In September, 1836, the Royal Bank of Ireland commenced business in Dublin with a subscribed capital of £1,500,000, taking over the business of Sir Robert Shaw, Bart., and Company, a firm of private bankers dating back from 1799. The bank had, at the time of its establishment, no branches, but some local branches have since been opened in Dublin. A portion of the shares (£14,000) was held at one time by the directors of the Agricultural Bank for the purpose of leading to a connection between the two banks, but the failure of the Agricultural Bank occurred, fortunately, before the negotiations were completed.

The Royal Bank did not possess the privilege of issuing notes, and a petition to the Chancellor of the Exchequer in 1844, for leave to register as a Bank of Issue, was met with a polite refusal. Until 1845 the law did not even permit Joint Stock Banks in Dublin to accept bills drawn at less than six months after date, nor to sue or be sued in the names of their public officers.

In the same year the proprietors annulled the clauses of the deed of settlement providing for the election of a portion of the directorate from among the English proprietary, a course said to be rendered necessary in consequence of the gradual transfer to Ireland of the greater portion of the shares held in England, originally a moiety of the whole paid-up capital.

In 1845 the minds of the directors appear to have been greatly exercised as to the propriety of the item of bank premises appearing in their statements of account. A resolution had been passed to the effect that this item had been reduced to £5,000, which amount was fully represented by the value of the premises, and any further reduction was prohibited. The directors, in 1845, submitted a proposition to rescind this resolution. Their object in calling attention to the matter was two-fold. "Firstly, by permitting the amount to be further reduced and ultimately extinguished, there will be removed from the balance sheet an asset, which, although having a *bona-fide* representative, possesses no banking availability; and secondly, until circumstances render it advisable to raise the dividend paid by the bank, there will be afforded a ready and natural outlet for the unappropriated surplus exhibited in the statement." An unlooked-for outlet was, however, afforded in 1848, when the surplus of £9,119 was appropriated to a bad and doubtful debt fund to meet losses, the major part of which had been created by the failure of a firm whose senior partner was a member of the Board.

In 1847 the bills negotiated during the year were stated to have amounted to £3,280,000 of which £1,500,000 were Irish, and the total losses were under £3,500.

The following figures indicate the progress which the bank has made :—

Years.	Paid-up Capital.	Dividend and Bonus for Year.	Reserve Fund.	Liabilities to Public.
	£	%	£	£
1837	208,750	5	3,380	—
1847	209,175	5	45,474	—
1857	209,175	14	77,000	951,365
1867	*300,000	16	215,000	1,535,390
1877	300,000	14½	200,000	1,977,244
1887	300,000	11	200,000	1,630,445
1888	300,000	11	200,000	1,772,767

The last competitor to enter the field, **The Munster and Leinster Bank,** was established in 1885, to supply the vacancy caused by the failure of the Munster Bank, in the banking accommodation of the South of Ireland. It commenced business on October 19th, occupying, by arrangement with the liquidators, the offices of the defunct Munster Bank in Cork, Dublin, and several of the country branches, and afterwards purchasing for £50,000 the premises in Cork, Dublin, and thirty-three out of the forty-one country branches. As the new bank has only been some four years in operation, its history has yet to be written, but the following extracts from the balance sheets presented, shew the extent of the success it has so far met with.

* The increase took place in 1864.

MUNSTER AND LEINSTER BANK, LIMITED.

	Dec., 1886.	Dec., 1887.	Dec., 1888.
	£	£	£
Paid up Capital	148,751	150,000	150,000
Reserve Fund	—	15,000	50,000
Liabilities to the Public	1,290,832	1,134,226	1,350,672
Dividends	3 %	5 %	6 %
Assets..................................	1,437.293	1,300,871	1,556.762
Net Profit for half year...........	5,016	6,134	7,825
Number of Branches	33	33	33

CHAPTER VIII.

Failed Banks.—The Agricultural and Commercial Bank of Ireland and the Southern Bank of Ireland.

Messrs. Mooney and Dwyer—Prestige derived from similarity of Directors' names with those of well-known merchants—Directors—Means adopted to secure shareholders—Branch Managers selected according to their holding of stock—Bills discounted for intending shareholders—Class from which shareholders were drawn—Chaos at the Branches—Absence of any system of book-keeping or inspection—Last Balance Sheet issued—Feeling of distrust created—Misunderstanding between the Board and Mr. Mooney—Position of antagonism taken up by Mr. Mooney—Election of Mr. Gresham as a Director—Request made to him to provide funds—Application to the Bank of Ireland for assistance—Further advances obtained through Mr. Gresham—Scene at the Meeting of Creditors—Resumption of business and second failure—Defect in the law relating to Joint Stock Companies—Mr. Mooney's subsequent career in Dublin, Melbourne and San Francisco—Formation of the Southern Bank of Ireland—Stoppage of payment—Commercial character of the proprietors.

VIEWED in relation to its effects and to the excitement it produced, the failure of the Agricultural and Commercial Bank of Ireland was the most prominent disaster in connection with Joint Stock Banking in Ireland. This ill-fated institution was founded in 1834, by a Mr. Thomas Mooney, a Dublin baker, who appealed to the patriotism of his countrymen to aid him in the formation of a bank of a truly national character. In this enterprise he was joined by Mr. James Dwyer, a gentleman, who for two years, "when he was a student in progress to becoming a barrister," had been Secretary to the Hibernian Bank, and who, having read "several of the treatises upon banking as matters of general information and curiosity" had thereby qualified himself for the position of Chairman.

Mr. Mooney was fortunate in the possession of a patronymic which also happened to be borne by another gentleman of great reputed wealth, residing at Pill Lane, Dublin, and he secured the services as a Director of Mr. James Chambers, a stationer of Abbey Street, whose name, singularly enough, was precisely the same as that of a Director of the Bank of Ireland—a man of considerable eminence and fortune. The similarity of these names was a circumstance of considerable value to the new institution. Everybody rushed to the conclusion that Mr. Mooney was his wealthy namesake of Pill Lane; and that Mr. Chambers was the Director of the Bank of Ireland, though the very fact of his being so would have seemed to render unlikely his acceptance of a similar position on the Board of a rival bank. Mr. T. M. Gresham, an unfortunate Director who joined the concern within a week of the failure, in entire ignorance of the position of affairs, in his evidence before the House of Commons Committee in 1837, said, "The fact is there is no manner of doubt that we were all deceived in two names in that bank, which were, Thomas Mooney and John Chambers; Thomas Mooney used to sign without putting his address, and I, myself, thought it was another Thomas Mooney, who is a gentleman of large property, of very high standing in society and a perfect man of business; and Mr. Chambers, who is a Director of the Bank of Ireland at this moment; we all thought it was him, North, South, East and West." Mr. Peirce Mahony in his evidence before the same Committee, said, "I was, myself, two years under the impression that one of the Directors, Mr. Mooney, was a merchant of the highest respectability in Dublin, and another, Mr. John Chambers, was also a merchant of high reputation; I know that that was not merely my error, but that of the public generally, and so great was the delusion that Mr. Gresham, before he became a member of the Board, thought he was to be associated with the two gentlemen I refer to, and when he came to the Board he found them two different men, though bearing the same names. Mr. Christie, one of the most respectable men in London, told me he was led astray in the very same manner." The remaining Directors were not of any particular note. They were:

Mr. Thomas Dixon, of Abbeyline, County Dublin; Mr. Scanlan; Mr. M'Gusty; Mr. Smith, of FitzWilliam Place; Mr. Kelly, of Tuam; Mr. Jones, of Dame Street, partner in the firm of Nott, Ferguson & Co., Tea Merchants.

Subsequently the Board was joined by Captain Childers, who was described as "a gentleman a little embarrassed," and who had been discharged as an insolvent debtor. Another Director, Mr. Tilly, becoming alarmed at the state of the bank retired in November, 1835, but rejoined the Board in 1836.

The capital of the bank was originally fixed at £1,000,000, upon which £1 per share was to be paid.* By this means it was designed to make the shares a means of investment for all sorts and classes of the people. But the response to the appeal of the promoters does not in the first instance appear to have been of a very encouraging character, judging from the circumstance that when the first branch was opened at Nenagh, Co. Tipperary, in November, 1834, the paid-up capital is alleged to have been less than £1,000, and admittedly did not exceed £3,000. It was, however, intimated that the directors would be prepared to treat liberally with the shareholders in the matter of discounts and loans, and as a further means of raising capital, it was decided that the qualification of the branch managers should be at least 300 shares, preference being given to applicants according to their holding of the bank's stock. Another method of filling up the subscription list, which was proved to have been resorted to, was to discount a bill, for from £5 to £10, for an intending shareholder, and to deduct from the proceeds £1 for the deposit on the share, with the idea, it was explained, "of embodying the agricultural population in the Bank." Under the influence of these and other inducements, and in view of the success attending the operations of the Northern and Provincial Banks, a large number of "patriots" eventually took up shares. At the date of the suspension over 250,000 shares had been issued, and the amount of the capital as adjusted by the auditors was £300,000 paid up. Mr. George Dundas, who was one of the auditors appointed by the Shareholders after the failure, stated in his examination before the House of Commons Committee in 1837 that in the town of Belfast alone there were 500 Shareholders, including a coach porter who withdrew 150 guineas from the Savings Bank and invested it in the bank's shares; a Street constable who had invested the savings of thirty years, amounting to £300, in a like manner, and many

* Subsequently fully paid shares of £10 were issued and also £25 shares with £10 paid.

young men in offices, linen lappers, and widows, etc., seeking a better investment for their money.

The Branch Managers were selected, as has been stated, solely according to their holding of the bank's stock, and without regard to their fitness to fulfil the duties required of them. The first Manager appointed was a country farmer. At the branches, matters seem to have been conducted at the will and pleasure of the officers, and wholly without regard to instructions from head quarters. Thus the Manager of the Cork branch is credited not only with having made advances to himself without security, but even with raising his own salary and that of the officials at the branch, and dating the increase back to the commencement of their engagements without any authority whatever from the Head Office. At one of the Northern Branches the Manager received notice that his services would not be required; as he declined to accept this notice, the Directors advertised his removal in the newspapers, and he retaliated by closing the Branch in the middle of business, and thus causing a violent panic.

But if chaos reigned at the branches, the position of affairs at the Head Office was equally unsatisfactory. During the greater part of the bank's existence, the attention of the staff was entirely directed to getting in money to meet runs which arose at different points, and the details of the business were left to take care of themselves. For four months before the stoppage, the books had not been posted. The minute books of the Board were not properly kept, and the attendance of members was irregular and uncertain. There was no system of inspection, and there was no register of notes. From some of the forty-six branches no returns had been made to the Head Office, in one case for so long as fourteen months, in another for six weeks, and their absence did not cause any remark. The auditors, in their report following the suspension of the bank, declared that "the book-keeping had been so faulty that they were convinced no accurate balance-sheet could at any time have been constructed," and the actual liabilities were only ascertained by public advertisements addressed to the note-holders and others. One of the auditors, Mr. Wm. Goodier, formerly Manager of the National Provincial Bank of England at Manchester, in his evidence before the House of Commons Committee in 1837, gave an account of his visits to some of the branches. At Kilkenny the books were not complete and the balances of bills and cash were incorrect. The contents of the till were represented by the Managers' I.O.U.'s and some forged notes. At Waterford and Limerick where there were local Boards of Directors, matters were in a more satisfactory state, but at Cork the book-keeping was irregular, and there had been gross peculation. The failure of the bank has, indeed, been ascribed to bad book-keeping, but it is evident that other elements of unsound banking also contributed to this result.

On 17th October, 1836, the following statement of account was submitted to the shareholders :—

LIABILITIES.	£ s. d.	£ s. d.
Paid-up Capital	375,029 15 0	
Notes in Circulation	421,596 15 0	
Deposits and Current Accounts	366,182 4 7	
Total Liabilities ...		1,162,808 14 7
ASSETS.		
Bills on hands	902,457 2 2	
Government and other Securities	20,607 6 11	
Property in Dublin and at the branches valued at	28,500 0 0	
Credit Account	93,731 11 9	
Cash on hands	134,892 5 11	
Total Assets		1,180,188 6 9
Surplus Assets		17,379 12 2
Five per cent. on the paid-up capital for the half year amounts to		9,375 0 0
		8,004 12 2
The Reserve Fund at last balance sheet was		5,741 16 11
Added this half year		2,262 15 3
Total to credit of Reserve Fund		£8,004 12 2

I certify the above to be correct according to the books of the Company.

JOHN MACKENZIE.

WM. HODGES.

JAMES DWYER.

J. CHAMBERS.

This balance sheet which was issued less than a month before the suspension, was accompanied by a statement calling attention to "the beneficial progress of a great national undertaking."

But in spite of these satisfactory assurances a feeling of distrust existed, both among depositors and holders of notes, in regard to the position of the bank. A "misunderstanding" had arisen between the Board and Mr. Mooney, the founder, who had appropriated to himself some scrip, representing shares in the Royal Bank, the property of the Agricultural Bank, standing in his name as a trustee. About the same time, unfortunately, the directors, viewing with alarm the lock up of their capital in unrealisable securities, were in treaty with a London Assurance Company, the Minerva (which has since disappeared), as to the investment of a portion of their capital in the stock of the Agricultural Bank. The energetic Mr. Mooney was then engaged in the promotion of an Irish Insurance Company, and saw in this arrangement a competition which would be disadvantageous to the interests of his new venture. He wrote, therefore, to the Irish newspapers, complaining that the Agricultural Bank was selling itself to English capitalists. This, and other indications, opened the eyes of the public to the fact that the condition of the bank was not so prosperous as it was represented to be, and under the influence of suspicions thus aroused, the pressure upon the institution began to be severe, and soon developed into a "run." Mr. Gresham was then asked to become a director, and having consented, he took his seat at the Board on November 8th, 1836. On the following day he was asked by his brother directors to procure funds, or the bank would stop, and he thereupon sold out his property in the funds, amounting to £8,000, and transferred that sum to the bank. On November 11th an application for assistance was made to the Bank of Ireland who offered the money required, on bills, provided that they were endorsed by Mr. Gresham. As he proved obdurate, an excuse was made to the Bank of Ireland, that Mr. Gresham had gone home, but that the whole of the directors, including the Lord Mayor of Dublin, would sign the bills and give the endorsement, and would also give a letter binding themselves personally. The commercial standing of the directors is evident from the circumstance that these terms were refused, and pressure was again put upon Mr. Gresham to induce him to put his name to the bills. Mr. Dwyer told him that he would give a great deal to be placed in such a proud situation, and that the salvation of the three countries was in his hands, to which Mr. Gresham replied that "he did not consider it a proud situation but a very melancholy one." Eventually he succumbed to the pressure put upon him, and the required advances were obtained. This, however, only delayed the collapse for three days, and the bank closed its doors on November 14th, 1836. The scene at the second meeting of creditors was described as being one of uproar and confusion, of fighting, swearing, and riot. The Lord Mayor of Dublin was assaulted, pulled off the platform, and compelled to obtain the protection of the city constables. Shareholders attended from all parts of the country. Two steamboats came from Belfast filled with proprietors, the majority of whom were persons in a humble position of life, and whose expenses were paid by the directors, or by subscription. Another contingent arrived from the South of Ireland in canal boats, and the confusion was so great that it was almost impossible to transact business. The deed of settlement contained a clause providing that the consent of the Board was necessary before the bank could be liquidated, and the directors availing themselves of this provision, again started business in opposition to the wishes of the body of proprietors. But public confidence was lost. The revelations made were of an unusually damaging character, and the bank again stopped payment in 1841.

A special Act of Parliament was necessary to wind up the affairs and received the Royal Assent in 1844.

A serious defect in the law, as it then stood, as regards the suing powers of shareholders *inter se* was, that there were no means of enforcing the provisions of the deed of settlement, or otherwise restraining misconduct by those entrusted with the management of a joint-stock company, except by the filing of a bill of equity, a most tortuous process which involved each of the shareholders being made parties to the suit. When the company was a large one, generations might pass away before a cause to which all were parties could be brought to a hearing, so that a judicial termination was totally impossible. Any omission of the name of a single shareholder invalidated the whole proceedings, and rendered the party suing liable to bear the whole costs incurred. If a shareholder disputed the insertion of his name on the register—and from the defective administration of the Act, and the fact that any person's name could be inserted as a shareholder without authority, this not unfrequently happened—a bill of equity was again necessary to determine the question, and the case delayed beyond all further proceeding. It there were any new shareholder, he had to be made a party, if a shareholder became bankrupt, the bill required amendment, in the event of death, the personal representatives of the deceased had to be substituted, and in cases where minors were partners, the fact had to be ascertained, and their guardians included. Thus, in the case of the Agricultural Bank, the directors were legally suspended according to their deed, and yet, notwithstanding the opinions of eminent counsel, they continued to act, and there was no possible remedy for the partners whose funds they held, and whose fortunes were responsible for all their acts, but a suit in equity, which would require the whole of some four thousand six hundred shareholders to be before the Court.* This defect in the law applied to England and Scotland, as well as to Ireland.

It is significant of the degree of confidence placed by the Irish in their banks, that Mr. Mooney, the founder of the Agricultural Bank, again started business as a banker in Dublin, under the style of the Provident Bank of Ireland, a title nearly resembling the Provincial Bank, and with notes similarly engraved.

He was again unfortunate, as his name appears in the list of bankrupts in 1840. Nothing daunted, however, Mr. Mooney left Ireland, and in due course appeared in Melbourne where he carried on his original calling of a baker, though on a very small scale. Nevertheless he succeeded within a few months in building, on credit, the National Hotel in Bourke Street, and the Princess' Theatre in Spring Street. He also stood as a candidate for the Colonial Parliament, but although he promised every citizen of Victoria a vote, a farm, and a rifle, he failed to secure election. He subsequently left Melbourne, and was next heard of in San Francisco where he started a "Mechanics' Bank" and after a brief interval absconded with the funds.

---

* Evidence of Mr. Peirce Mahony before the House of Commons Committee, 1837.

The Southern Bank of Ireland, a bank of issue, was established in 1837 on the ashes of the Cork business of the Agricultural Bank. The nominal capital was £500,000 with power of extension to £1,000,000. The Manager was Mr. William Mitchell, formerly Manager of the Agricultural Bank, and he was joined by the local manager and accountant of the Agricultural Bank's Branch at Cork. Mr. Mitchell was previously with the Western Bank of Scotland, so that his banking experience was an unusually unfortunate one. The Southern Bank, however, soon stopped payment, probably from the exposure of its affairs in the evidence taken before the House of Commons Committee in the same year, after a very brief existence of some two months.

Mr. Peirce Mahony referring to the bank in his evidence before that Committee said :—

"I have looked to the register of that bank. I know the City of Cork, and the commercial character of parties there, probably as well as most persons, and I do not hesitate to state to this Committee that the registry at the Stamp-Office in Dublin by that Company, exhibits the grossest possible abuse of the Act of Parliament under which it professes to act. I do not believe there are above 40 or 50 persons registered as shareholders. I do not believe a deed of any kind exists ; and as to the credit of those parties, I should be very sorry to take £500 endorsed by the whole of them."

CHAPTER IX.

The Tipperary Joint Stock Bank.

Establishment and Directors—Issue of Bank of Ireland Notes—Business and profits—Failure in 1856—John Sadleir's letter to his brother—His career —Rapid rise—His speculations and embarrassments—Purchase of the business of the Newcastle Commercial Bank—John Sadleir's suicide and defalcations.

THE Tipperary Joint Stock Bank was founded on the business of Scully's Private Bank in 1838, by Mr. John Sadleir. The Directors were John Sadleir and his brother James, and Mr. James Scully, who died in 1846, and was succeeded by Mr. Vincent Scully. Subsequently the name of Mr. Wilson Kennedy appeared as a Director. The bank did not issue its own notes, but discounted with the Bank of Ireland paper under a special arrangement; the power was, however, reserved to it by a clause in the Act of 1845; to take the same amount of issue as it would have been entitled to, in the event of the agreement with the Bank of Ireland coming to an end. Referring to this feature in their sixth Annual Report, the Directors said:—

"The success of the Tipperary Bank, conducted on this principle, seems to shew that it is not unadapted to Ireland, where the existing banks of issue have all, in the early years of their existence, been subjected to several severe and general runs on their branches by which they must have suffered great losses. The general failure of the old private country banks of Ireland (all but two or three) before 1822 or 1823, produced a want of confidence in any notes but those of the Bank of Ireland, which, however, the stability of the Joint Stock Banks since established, notwithstanding these runs, has pretty well done away with."

The business of the bank appears to have been comparatively a large one, and was carried on at Tipperary, Clonmel, Roscrea,

Carrick-on-Suir, Carlow, Athy and Thomastown. The capital was stated as £100,000, a portion of which was held by English proprietors.

At the close of each year, reports of the usual congratulatory character were submitted to the shareholders, dividends of six, eight, and nine per cent. were regularly divided among them, and surplus profits carried to Reserve or Contingency Funds. In the Report for 1844, the bad debts were, with praiseworthy precision, stated to amount to £617 4*s.* 9*d.*, and after payment of a dividend of 8 per cent., the very respectable sum of £6,271 was carried to Reserve. In their Report for 1846, we find the Directors deploring the distress caused by the potato famine, and announcing that they had given £115 9*s.* to the funds of the local Relief Committees. In 1847 the discounts were said to have exceeded a million pounds sterling without a single bill remaining unpaid. The final Report bears date of January, 1856, when a dividend and bonus equal to 9 per cent. per annum was declared, and the Reserve Fund was represented to amount to £17,375 12*s.* 10*d.*

There was thus everything to inspire confidence. The Directors were men well known, occupying high public positions, and identified with the locality in which the operations of the bank were conducted. The surprise of the proprietors and the public can therefore well be imagined, when in February, 1856, less than a month after the issue of a highly coloured Report and almost before the ink on the Dividend Warrants was dry, the doors of the bank were closed. The statement of affairs showed a deficiency exceeding £400,000—the greater part of which had been used by John Sadleir, with the connivance of his brother James, in gigantic speculations.

Taken in conjunction with the last Report quoted above, the following letter, addressed to James Sadleir by his brother, will be interesting as shewing how the fallacious figures were arrived at. It bears date "London, December 31st, 1855," a few weeks previous to the final collapse.

THE TIPPERARY JOINT STOCK BANK.

My Dear James,

The Accounts should be made out treating the paid-up capital as £100,000 on the 31st December, 1854; therefore the requisite number of shares to make this account square should be entered as vested in A. Ferrall, Esq., and he should be debited accordingly in an account in respect of the shares.

The "Reserve Fund" should be treated as £14,072 0*s.* 3*d.* on the 31st of December, 1854.

It will not be requisite to print and circulate among the Irish shareholders a balance-sheet, but as all the English shareholders are in the habit of getting from every bank in which they hold shares, a printed balance-sheet each half year, we must give them a printed balance-sheet at least once a year, and for the year ending the 31st of December, 1855.

By this means the present English shareholders will double their present holdings in the Tipperary Bank and I dare say, the balance of the £100,000 of Stock will be quickly taken up.

* * * * * * *

I enclose you the figures I gave Law (*i.e.*, Farmer John Law) and some few others, and the balance-sheet for the year ending the 31st of December, 1855, should be framed so as to tally with this balance-sheet for the year ending the 31st of December, 1854.

An increase of about £30,000 in the item of customers' balances, etc., should be made to appear. The item "trade fixtures" should be increased or decreased as you considered best.

The way to shew the customers' balances up to say £759,223 16*s.* 2*d.* or thereabouts, would be, of course, by crediting certain accounts—deposit or current accounts or both—and debiting certain other accounts for sums which in the whole would represent the same.

For example, six or seven deposit receipts may be issued to me for such and such sums, amounting in the whole to £400,000 or £500,000, and then four or five accounts might be opened such as :—

1. The South Eastern Swiss Railway Company.........£163,000
2. The Prussian Coal Company...............................£157,000
3. The Rome and Frascati Railway Company............£36,000
4. The Grand Junction Railway Company...............£48,000
5. The East Kent Railway Company.........................£157,000

£561,000

And each of the foregoing accounts might be debited with advances made to me as representing each of the said companies to the extent of the sums I set opposite each of the five accounts, and which sums would amount in all to £561,000.

Then the deposit receipts for £21,500 granted to the Backhouses might be added, and I should be debited with the said sum in an account called "John Sadleir, trustee in the Backhouse Mortgage."

All the foregoing accounts would be looked on as so many trust accounts obtained by arranging to advance as much as was received; and as the bank could not be called on to pay any of the deposit receipts so long as one penny was due on any of the accounts, the safety of the bank was perfect, and the question of interest both ways could be so adjusted as to work out enough of profit to enable the bank to pay the 6 per cent. interest and the 3 per cent. bonus on the £100,000 and to carry to the reserve fund a good sum—say £5,000.

I hope you will see this matter in the light I do; perhaps I have not sufficiently explained the case, but I am sure I am right and that the whole thing can be so managed as to defy any criticism, if such should be started, but of course, we should not court any. When I go over I can explain all. The books should be kept open for the requisite entries

*** * * * * * * ***

Yours affectionately,
(Signed) JOHN SADLEIR.

The career of John Sadleir, his rapid rise and tragic end, is one of the most remarkable episodes in Irish banking, and deserves more than passing notice. This "Prince of Swindlers," as he has been aptly designated, was trained for the law, and his first appearance was as a solicitor in Dublin, where he had succeeded to his uncle's practice and influential connection. In 1846 he relinquished his Irish business, and, when the railway mania was at its height, came over to London to establish himself as a Parliamentary agent, in which capacity he earned considerable repute and much profit, owing to his success in piloting through Parliament several important railway bills. In the following year he was elected Member of Parliament for Carlow, for which borough he sat until 1855. Before long, his character and talents began to attract attention in the House, and, upon the accession of Lord Aberdeen to the Premiership, he was offered, and accepted office as a Junior Lord of the Treasury. In the commercial world, where tales of his great wealth had been diligently propagated by his friends and followers, he had been for some time regarded as a financial luminary, and when to this already-established reputation was added the dignity of a legislator, and the membership of a powerful Administration, invitations to extend his name and influence to various joint stock companies flowed in freely upon him. He became chairman of the London and County Bank in 1848, chairman of the Royal Swedish Railway, and director of numerous other companies. In the Tipperary

Bank, though he was not, for some time preceding the failure, a director, he reigned supreme, and it was there that he was enabled to commence that career of fraud which ended so disastrously to the bank and to himself.

It is a curious circumstance, but one which finds a frequent parallel in the annals of crime, that, in the very zenith of his prosperity, and with brilliant opportunities open to him, John Sadleir should have first embraced a course fraught with such dangerous consequences. Yet he had been but a few months in office when rumours became current, which were soon confirmed by his resignation, that the new Junior Lord had been availing himself of the resources of the Treasury to foster some of his financial schemes. This was followed by his resignation of the chairmanship of the London and County Bank, and, though it was sought to put the best possible complexion on both these occurrences, suspicions were aroused in monetary circles as to whether the reputed wealth of John Sadleir was an existing quantity, and, if so, how it was represented.

Meanwhile, Sadleir had been using the funds of the Tipperary Bank in speculations in German coal mines, gold mines in California, and other wild schemes, until the bank had practically run dry, and it became necessary to resort to other means to obtain supplies. He then turned his attention to the Royal Swedish Railway Company, in which, as chairman, he was omnipotent, and he succeeded, by issuing duplicate shares, and by negotiating, for his own purposes, acceptances of the company, in mulcting the unfortunate shareholders to the extent of nearly £350,000. When practising as a solicitor in Dublin, he had made some successful speculations in the Irish Encumbered Estates Court, and in this way had become possessed of some of the seals of the Court. These he affixed to forged documents, and, as a further means of raising money, he deposited them as security for advances. More money was, however, required, and unfortunately at a time when the events just related, and the want of confidence which they engendered, rendered Sadleir's position one of considerable difficulty. A renewed attempt to pledge forged title deeds threw doubts on the genuineness of those already held by the same parties, and thus not only closed the door to further advances, but rendered imminent the detection of previous frauds. Still it was urgently necessary to find more money for his own requirements, and to meet the even more pressing necessities of the Tipperary Bank, where his overdraft without security amounted to no less than £200,000.

It happened about this time that the shareholders of the Newcastle-on-Tyne Commercial Banking Company desired to be relieved of their liability, and with this view, after having unsuccessfully tried to negotiate a sale of their business to the Royal British Bank, they approached the Sadleirs. The Newcastle bank was a small but respectable country institution, established in 1836. An average dividend of 6 per cent. had been paid since the commencement of business, and the capital of £50,000 was safe and intact. The only reason assigned for the determination arrived at was the illness of the managing director, which had deprived him of the use of his limbs. An agreement was hastily entered into between the Sadleirs and the directors of the Newcastle bank to purchase the share capital at par, and in pursuance of an arrangement made, assets amounting to upwards of £50,000 were sent to London, and employed in meeting the liabilities of the Tipperary Bank. Very little of this money, it may be added, found its way back to the confiding proprietary of the Newcastle bank. But it was wholly insufficient for the purpose, and, on the 13th February, 1856, after renewed efforts to obtain funds, the bills of the Tipperary Bank were returned by their London agents, Messrs. Glyn & Co.

The rest of Sadleir's story is soon told. Early on the morning of 17th February, 1856, a labouring man, crossing over Hampstead Heath, saw, at the back of "Jack Straw's Castle," a body lying on the ground, and beside it a silver cream jug, and a bottle labelled "poison." Its identity with John Sadleir was soon established, while letters addressed to his friends, the failure of the bank, and the concurrent discovery of his enormous and various frauds, left no doubt as to the reasons which impelled him to take his own life. After a lengthened inquiry, the jury returned a verdict of *felo de se.* One of his last letters, addressed to Mr. Keating, M.P. for Waterford, was produced at the inquest, and was in these terms :—

"No one has been privy to my crimes ; they sprung from my own cursed brain alone. I have swindled and deceived without the knowledge of any one. Stevens and Norris are both innocent, and have no knowledge of the fabrication of deeds and forgeries by me, and by which I have sought to go on, in the horrid hope of retrieving. It was a sad day for all when I came to London. I can give but little aid to unravel accounts and transactions."

It remains only to be added that his total defalcations exceeded a million and a quarter sterling, and that he left behind him a legacy of litigation which occupied the courts and the lawyers for many years after.

Many of the shareholders were ruined by the failure of the bank. Some seized all the property they could, and fled to America. James Sadleir absconded.

In August, 1881, a sum of £3,000 remained due to 647 creditors, who were required by an advertisement in the newspapers of August 12, 1881, to come forward and prove their claims prior to Jan. 11, 1882.

CHAPTER X.

UNSUCCESSFUL BANKS.—THE LONDON AND DUBLIN BANK, THE UNION BANK OF IRELAND, THE ENGLISH AND IRISH, THE EUROPEAN, AND THE MUNSTER BANKS.

The London and Dublin Bank—Scope of operations—Merits of the Bank—Memorial for permission to issue Notes—Importance attached to the privilege of issuing Notes—Feeling of Shareholders—Progress of the Bank—Closing in 1848—Necessity that any new bank should appeal to some specified class or sect—Banking and Politics—Union Bank of Ireland—Formation and Branches—Progress of business—Subsequent difficulties and liquidation—English and Irish Bank—First Report—Want of capital—Transfer of the business to the European Bank—Unexpected losses—European Bank—Dublin Branch opened in 1864, and closed in the following year—Munster Bank—Establishment—Directors—Rumours of borrowings by Directors—Litigation—Panic and Suspension—Frauds of Farquharson—Results of liquidation—Final Report of Liquidators.

THE London and Dublin Bank, an unsuccessful institution, commenced business in 1843, with a Head Office in London, and branches at Dublin, Dundalk, Wicklow, Mullingar, Kells, Parsonstown, and Carrick-on-Shannon. The capital was £260,000, to be paid up by 220 shareholders.

The bank was formed, as a non-issuing institution, to compete with the Bank of Ireland, in the Dublin circle, from which the issuing banks were then excluded. The National Bank had attempted to invade it at some points, by opening branches at which notes of the Bank of Ireland were issued, but had been compelled to withdraw. As the operations of the Royal and the Hibernian Banks were then confined to the capital, the whole of the counties lying within the fifty mile radius were without any banking accommodation whatever, and the want of it was alleged to have been much felt by merchants and traders.

The merits of the bank were stated to be that it was not a bank of issue, and was consequently less exposed to runs or panics; that power was vested in the honorary directors, being shareholders, in conjunction with the auditors elected by the shareholders, to dissolve the bank without the concurrence of the executive directors in the event of one-third of the subscribed capital being lost, and a power was vested in the shareholders also, to dissolve the bank upon proof of such a loss having been incurred; that the number of branches was limited, and that the bank was perfectly free from sect or party.

The first branch was opened at Dundalk on the compulsory withdrawal of the National Bank from that town. On the passing of the Act of 1845, the directors memorialised the Premier for permission to register as a bank of issue, on the ground that the removal of the exclusive privileges enjoyed up to that time by the Bank of Ireland, would bring the other banks possessing note issues to Dublin. Similar steps were taken by the Hibernian Bank and the Royal Bank of Ireland, but the requests were refused by Sir Robert Peel, who pointed out that the issues of the banks were fixed and could not be increased in consequence of any extension of branches which they might contemplate. It is evident, notwithstanding the advantages of non-issue claimed in the prospectus of the bank, that the possession of a note-issue was greatly coveted. Almost an undue importance seems to have been attached to this privilege, but it is in part accounted for by the profit to be derived from it. The cost of issuing notes was estimated at from 1½ to 2 per cent., while the current rate for loans was 6 per cent.*

At the second annual meeting, in 1846, one of the shareholders moved, as an amendment to the Report, that it was desirable to remove the head office to Dublin, as one-third of the paid-up capital, then amounting to £58,900, was held in Ireland. As this reason for making such a radical change seemed somewhat inadequate, he added that "through his advice many shareholders had joined the concern

* Estimates of Messrs. Robert Murray and Thomas Wilson, *Bankers' Magazine*, Vol. I., p. 63.

and he felt that he had unconsciously betrayed them, as he had informed them that every facility would be afforded for discounts." This argument seems to have satisfied the meeting that the existing arrangement had better not be disturbed, and the amendment was not carried.

But the bank made little progress. From the few figures available, it appears that in the first two years of its existence the net profits amounted to £2,305 and £4,131 respectively, sufficient to pay dividends of 4 per cent. on the capital then paid up. The *raison d'être* of the bank was removed by the passing of the Act of 1845, and it was closed in 1848, the National Bank taking over all the branches and thus re-entering the district from which, five years earlier, they had been compelled to retire. Three of the directors, viz.:—Sir Ralph Howard, Bart., M.P., Mr. Octavius Ommaney and Mr. Francis Carnac Brown joined the the Board of the latter institution. A call of £2 per share was made on the unfortunate proprietors.

It was an element of success with any new bank that it should have some party cry or appeal to some particular and specified class. The Bank of Ireland was considered the bank of the Protestants. The Hibernian Bank was established to grant the same facilities to the Roman Catholics. Both the Agricultural and the National Banks appealed to the patriotism of the Irish, an appeal which contributed greatly to the rapid progress of their business in its early stages. The London and Dublin Bank urged, as a special feature, that it was to be entirely free from any sect or party, and the result of its operations proved that it failed to enlist the influence or sympathy of either. It is evident that a great deal of feeling of this kind still exists, and it found expression so recently as the 11th February, 1889, when at a meeting of the Hibernian Bank, in Dublin, a motion was brought forward that Mr. R. W. Kelly, a retiring director, be not re-elected, because he had attended a banquet given in honour of Mr. Balfour, the chief secretary to the Lord-Lieutenant of Ireland. Mr. Kelly said he attended the banquet in his private capacity only, and had not authorised any one to describe him as the representative of the bank. This explanation was accepted, and Mr. Kelly was re-elected.

The Union Bank of Ireland was founded in 1862, with a nominal capital of £1,000,000. More than a quarter of a century had elapsed since any new bank had been started in Ireland, and it was thought, in view of the improved condition of the country, that there was a profitable opening for capital in this direction. The Head Office was in London, and there were branches at Cork, Limerick, Bray, Charleville, Kells, Abbeyleix, Fethard, Bruff and Kilmallock. The extent and progress of the business will be seen from the following figures :—

Half-year ended.	Capital paid-up.	Reserve Fund.	Dividend.	Net Profits.	Deposits.
	£	£	%	£	£
Dec., 1863	219,405	—	—	3,302	146,281
" 1864	220,000	2,000	4¼	5,914	366,480
" 1865	220,000	3,000	2½	5,247	423,810
" 1866	220,000	4,500	2	4,095	353,018

Until the end of 1865 a fair rate of progress was maintained, and the permanence of the institution seeming to be assured, a lease of nine hundred and ninety-nine years was taken of the offices in Dublin. But in the first half of 1866, the net profits, under the influence of the monetary crisis and Fenian difficulties of that year, fell to £541, and there was no dividend. In the latter half of 1866 there was a partial recovery, but in a subsequent half-year a loss of £13,000 was incurred. These unpleasant experiences resulted in the voluntary liquidation of the Bank in 1868, when the southern branches were purchased by the Munster Bank, and Dublin, and some of the Leinster branches by the Hibernian Bank.

The English and Irish Bank was established in 1863, with a nominal capital of £2,000,000, on the business of Robert Gray and Co., private bankers in Dublin. The head office of the bank was in London. According to the first report the paid-up capital was £75,320, the deposits were £256,485, the gross profits £9,298, and the net profits £1,997. Owing, it was alleged, to want of capital, the progress made was not as rapid as was expected, and an arrangement was therefore concluded in 1864 with the European Bank, for the purchase of the business, the proprietors receiving shares in the

European, in exchange for their holdings. Though the English and Irish Bank was only a few months in existence, a considerable loss was incurred. At the final meeting, the late Sir Robert W. Carden, who was in the chair, stated that, in liquidating their resources, they were confronted with an unexpected deficiency amounting to about £8,000, which the directors had determined to meet themselves. Four of the directors joined the Board of the European Bank.

The European Bank opened a Dublin Office in 1864, but retired in 1865 when the business was transferred to the Munster Bank. The European Bank was originally the Union Bank of England and France, and the name was changed on the subsequent absorption of the London and Netherlands Bank. It had a very short career, as it liquidated voluntarily in 1866.

The Munster Bank, Limited, originally the National Investment Company, Limited, was established in Cork, in 1864, the chief field of its operations being in the south of Ireland until 1870, when it absorbed the business of Messrs. La Touche and Co., of Dublin. The nominal capital was £1,000,000, increased to £1,500,000 in 1880, of which £525,000 was paid up, and at the time of the suspension, the reserve fund was stated to amount to £200,000. The bank was registered under the Companies' Acts, 1862 and 1879, and the reserve liability of the proprietors was £750,000. The following were directors when the bank closed its doors :—Nicholas D. Murphy, D.L., Cork, Edmund G. Dease, Rath-house, Queen's County, Joseph W. M'Mullen, J.P., Cork, James J. Murphy, Lady's Well Brewery, Cork, William Lumley Perrier, J.P., Cork, John Warren Payne, J.P., Bantry.

For many years the business appears to have been of an extensive and profitable character. Dividends of from 6 to 12 per cent. were paid, and according to the last report, issued in January, 1885, the liabilities to the public amounted to £2,466,461, the assets to £3,328,172, and the profit for the half-year to £30,212, including £5,605 12*s.* 1*d.* brought forward. Its troubles commenced about two years before the final collapse, when rumours began to circulate that the directors were lending the bank's money to themselves, on insufficient security, or no security at all, and some of the shareholders, becoming alarmed, instituted legal proceedings. The action against Mr. Wm. Shaw, M.P. for the County of Cork, the former chairman, was compromised, but the case against another director was proceeded with. It transpired in the course of this litigation, that, upon security for £51,898, advances amounting to £145,190 had been made to Mr. Shaw and the firms of which he was a partner, while Mr. D. Murphy, another director, received advances of £23,103, on security valued at £8,995. Nor was this policy confined to the dealings of the directors with themselves. A Mr. Delany, of Cork, who had failed, admitted in cross-examination that he received advances of from £20,000 to £30,000, upon security worth only £5,000. In giving judgment, holding the defendant directors all liable for advances made in direct contravention to the Articles of Association, the Vice-Chancellor of Ireland said that in his opinion "there had been systematic and fraudulent appropriation of the property of the bank, extending over a period of years." As the result of these revelations a feeling of uneasiness seized depositors; a steady run set in, and on the evening of July 14th, 1885, the bank suspended payment. The official announcement was as follows:—

"The directors announce with deep regret that the bank has been obliged to suspend payment, owing to the large and continued withdrawals of deposits since the recent litigation in the Vice-Chancellor's Court in the case of 'Jackson *v.* the Munster Bank.' In making the announcement the directors think it right to add that on a careful realisation they expect the securities held by the bank will be amply sufficient to discharge its liabilities."

This expectation, which usually accompanies announcements of this kind, was not realised. An examination of the books, after the failure, disclosed the existence of fraud on the part of Robert Farquharson, one of the joint managers at Dublin, who by gambling on the Stock Exchange, and living in a style far beyond his means, had succeeded in mulcting the proprietors to the extent of £70,000. Farquharson absconded and has not since been heard of.

The liquidation commenced on September 12th, 1885, and was completed in January, 1889. The following details are extracted from the final report of the liquidators.

"The creditors of the bank numbered about 19,000, and the liabilities amounted to £2,674,370 19*s.* 1*d.* Of this amount £508,748 16*s.* 5*d.* was due to the Bank of Ireland and the Union Bank of London, both of which were fully secured. These secured debts were paid off, and the securities released within the first three months of the liquidation. Leave was obtained from the court at a later date to pay off in full all claims of £15 and under. Altogether in the first year of the liquidation claims to the amount of £529,136 18*s.* 10*d.* were paid in full.

"The claims of unsecured creditors admitted by the liquidators before the end of the first year amounted to £1,938,912 19*s.* 10*d.* On this amount a dividend of ten shillings in the pound was declared on the 31st March, and a second, of five shillings in the pound, on the 29th September, 1886, the two amounting together to £1,454,184 14*s.* 10*d.*, and making, with the sum already mentioned as paid to the secured creditors and on £15 claims, a total sum of close on two millions sterling made available for distribution to the creditors of the bank within fifteen months from its stoppage.

"The whole of these dividends were paid, on behalf of the liquidators, by the Munster and Leinster Bank, through their thirty-three offices, without the occurrence of any hitch or delay. When it is considered that on each occasion some 15,000 separate creditors had to be dealt with, this result is highly creditable to the manner in which the business was carried through by them.

"The nominal value of the assets of the bank at the time of its suspension was £3,435,431 1*s.* 5*d.*; but it early became apparent that the real value of these assets was insufficient, taking into consideration the necessary delay and expense of their realization, to pay off the creditors within a reasonable time, and the liquidators, therefore, deemed it their duty to make a call of £2 per share on the shareholders of the company, payable in two instalments of £1 each, on the 10th March and the 9th June, 1886. On the 150,000 shares in the company, this call amounted to £300,000. There was actually realized out of it, previous to the transfer of the assets to the Munster and Leinster Bank, Limited, on the 17th November, 1886, £206,389 1*s.* 4*d.* The shareholders numbered about 3,800.

"The Munster and Leinster Bank, Limited, was formed chiefly by shareholders in the Munster Bank, Limited, soon after the suspension of the bank, and was registered as a limited company on the 19th September, 1885. It commenced business on the 19th October, occupying, by arrangement with the liquidators, the offices in Cork, Dublin, and several of the country branches, and, on the 19th December, a bargain was concluded for the sale, to the Munster and Leinster Bank, for £50,000, of the premises and furniture in Cork, Dublin, and thirty out of the forty-one country branches of the Bank.

"From the establishment of the new bank, great assistance was rendered by it to the liquidators, both by the purchase of a considerable number of accounts, and by the collection of debts in the country branches. By this means the payment of the earlier dividends was materially accelerated.

"Dividends amounting to fifteen shillings in the pound on the admitted claims, as well as the full amount of all claims of £15 and under, having been provided for, and all the secured debts of the bank having been paid, there remained at the end of the first year of the liquidation a liability of five shillings in the pound on the claims admitted to the end of the first year, amounting to £484,728 5*s.*, and on claims subsequently admitted, amounting, as estimated, to about £6,250. The remaining assets, by the best tests which could be applied to them, were valued at £639,761 19*s.* 3*d.*

"This estimate showed an apparent surplus, provided the realization could be spread over a sufficient space of time, of rather less than £149,000.

"On the other hand, it was evident that most of the best assets having been realized, the future work of the liquidation must necessarily be attended with a very much greater proportionate cost than what had already been accomplished. On such a forced realization as would have been incumbent on the liquidators, the proceeds of the remaining assets were certain to fall very far short of the estimate, while extensive and very troublesome legal proceedings would have been necessary if the outstandings were to be collected within any reasonable time.

"Under these circumstances, it was with feelings of much relief that the liquidators received from the directors of the Munster and Leinster Bank, Limited, a proposal to take over the whole of the remaining assets of the bank, on the condition of their paying off the remaining liabilities.

"This proposal resulted in an agreement, entered into on the 25th September, 1886, which, having been accepted as a compromise by the creditors of the bank, in the manner provided by 'The Joint Stock Companies Act, 1870,' and unanimously approved by the shareholders, was, on the 17th November, sanctioned by an order of the Master of the Rolls.

"By this agreement, the liquidators sold to the Munster and Leinster Bank, Limited, all the assets and property of the bank, of every kind whatsoever, then remaining in their hands, including the amount remaining unpaid of the call of £2 per share made on the contributories, and the Munster and Leinster Bank became responsible for all the remaining debts and liabilities of the bank, agreeing to indemnify the Munster Bank, its shareholders, and the liquidators against all future claims or demands whatsoever, and undertook to pay the remaining 5*s.* in the £ due to the creditors, by two instalments of 2*s.* 6*d.* each, with interest at 1 per cent. per annum, within six and twelve months respectively from the date of the sanction of the agreement by the Court. By a subsequent arrangement these instalments were made payable respectively on the 7th May and the 7th November, 1887.

"No difficulty or delay arose in carrying out the agreement, and on or before the dates mentioned the dividend was placed within the reach of every creditor of the bank who was not incapacitated by some sort of legal disability, such as existed in the cases of minors or lunatics, or where there was no legal personal representative of a deceased creditor, or where a creditor had removed in such a way as that he could not be traced. Besides the limited number of cases in which payment has thus been hitherto impracticable, there remain a certain number of creditors who, though duly placed in possession of their dividend cheques, have not, up to the present time, taken the trouble to present them for payment. The whole result of this operation has, however, been very satisfactory, and the amount of liability now remaining undischarged is exceedingly small.

"As the work was substantially completed by the distribution of the final instalment, made 7th November, 1887, it may be said that the whole liabilities of the bank, amounting to considerably over two millions and a half sterling, were discharged within two years and a half from its suspension, placing the liquidators in a position, within three years and a half from their appointment, to report that the affairs of the Company are fully wound up, and to apply for the dissolution of the Company and for their own discharge.

"The total expenses of the liquidation disbursed by the liquidators from the commencement were as follows :—

	£	s.	d.
First year	£38,849	11	10
Second year	22,901	8	9
Third year	504	19	4
Since end of third year	15	0	0
Total	£62,270	19	11

"This total is made up of the following items, viz. :—

	£	s.	d.
Salaries—chiefly paid previous to the date of Transfer to Munster and Leinster Bank	**£17,292**	**1**	**2**
Commission paid Munster and Leinster Bank on Collections and Dividends	**3,554**	**0**	**0**
Law Costs	**11,121**	**11**	**5**
Liquidators' Remuneration	**15,000**	**0**	**0**
General Charges, including Rents, Rates and Taxes, Accountants' Remuneration and Expenses, Costs of Valuations, Travelling Expenses, &c., &c. ...	**15,303**	**7**	**4**
	£62,270	**19**	**11**

"As the amount of cash which passed through the liquidation accounts, as shown by the abstract at foot, was £2,104,907 0*s*. 1*d*., it will be seen that the expenses amounted to rather less than 3 per cent. on the amount realized, a result largely due, as already pointed out, to the effective assistance rendered in the early stages of the liquidation by the Munster and Leinster Bank, and still more to their having taken over so large a proportion of accounts which would have been slow and difficult of realization, before any serious expense had been incurred in connection with them.

"The work of the liquidation was much facilitated throughout by the careful judicial supervision exercised over it by the Right Hon. the Master of the Rolls, and by the kindly consideration which he gave to every matter in which application was made to him for guidance or instruction.

"In order more effectually to vest in the Munster and Leinster Bank, Limited, the assets transferred to them by the agreement already referred to, and to facilitate their future dealings with the property and accounts of the bank, it was deemed advisable to obtain an Act of Parliament confirming the agreement. By an Order of the Court, made 13th December, 1886, the liquidators were empowered to join with the directors of the Munster and Leinster Bank in promoting the Bill for this purpose. The Act was passed through Parliament without any difficulty, and received the Royal Assent on the 28th April, 1887.

"The expense of obtaining this Act, which amounted to £1,090 15*s.* 9*d.*, was borne by the Munster and Leinster Bank, and is not, therefore, included in the accounts of the liquidators.

* * * * * *

"From the date of the filing of this certificate the control of the liquidators over any part whatever of the capital or assets of the Munster Bank, Limited, has absolutely and finally ceased. As regards the contributories of the bank, any balance still unpaid on the call of £2 per share made by the liquidators remains due to the Munster and Leinster Bank as fully and effectually as it was formerly due to the liquidators; but it is no longer in the power either of the liquidators or of the Munster and Leinster Bank, Limited, to make any further call, under any circumstances whatever. The property of the Munster Bank, Limited, and the accounts still due to it, are now absolutely vested in and due to the Munster and Leinster Bank, Limited, while as regards the creditors of the Munster Bank, Limited, if any liabilities still remain outstanding for which claims have not yet been admitted, such liabilities are now liabilities of the Munster and Leinster Bank, Limited, and may be proved against it in the same way as previous to the passing of the Act they might have been proved against the Munster Bank, Limited.

"The winding-up of the Munster Bank, Limited, being thus complete, and the duties and responsibilities of the liquidators terminated, nothing remains but the dissolution of the company, for which purpose a resolution will be submitted to you.

JAMES J. MURPHY, } *Liquidators.*
FREDERICK W. PIM, }

CORK, 12*th January*, 1889.

D. and T. FITZGERALD, *Solicitors*,
Dublin;

FREDERICK HALL, *Solicitor*,
Cork.

GENERAL ABSTRACT OF ACCOUNTS.

Dr.	£	s.	d.	Cr.	£	s.	d.
To Cash received on Account of Current Accounts, Bills, Loans, Interest, &c.	1,898,517	18	9	By Accounts paid in full	529,136	18	10
,, Cash received on Account of Calls ...	206,389	1	4	,, Dividends paid previous to transfer of Assets and liabilities to Munster and Leinster Bank, Limited, on claims admitted by Liquidators ...	1,470,705	1	2
				,, Up-keep of Estate and securities, and Premiums paid on Policies held as security	20,840	19	0
				,, Expenses of Liquidation	62,270	19	11
				,, Cash transferred to Munster and Leinster Bank, Limited	16,902	15	0
				,, Final balance of Cash to be paid over to Munster and Leinster Bank, Ltd. ...	5,050	6	2
	£2,104,907	0	1		£2,104,907	0	1

CHAPTER XI.

The Irish Banking Act.

The Act 8 and 9 Victoria — Provisions — Average circulation — Union of banks—Relinquishment of issue—Prohibition of fractional notes—Bank of Ireland privileges—Present position of the bank—Authorised issues—Operation of the Act—Law relating to payment of notes—Large holding of specie by Irish banks—Doubt as to Bank of England notes being legal tender in Ireland.

THE year 1845 saw the final legislative effort to regulate banking in Ireland, the 8 and 9 Victoria, cap. 37, of which the chief provision was the removal of all restrictions on banks carrying on business and issuing notes in Dublin or within fifty miles thereof. The following is an epitome of the principal provisions of the Act :—

No banker should issue more than the average amount of his circulation during the period of one year preceding the 1st May, 1845, according to the returns made, in pursuance of the Act, 4 and 5 Victoria, c. 50.

For any excess over this amount, gold and silver coin must be held in a proportion not exceeding one quarter of silver to that of gold, at the principal offices or depots, not exceeding four in number.

In case of the union of two or more banks, the new bank may issue to the amount of the circulation of the united banks. In this respect it may be remarked that the law is similar to that of Scotland, but differs from that of England.

On a bank relinquishing its issue, the Bank of Ireland was authorised to increase its issue by the amount relinquished. (The Bank of England can only issue to the extent of two-thirds in a similar case.) Each bank was required to render weekly accounts to the Commissioners of Stamps and Taxes, distinguishing the notes below £5, and the amount of coin held at each of the head offices, or principal places of issue.

The issue of notes for fractional sums, and for amounts under twenty shillings, was prohibited. The withdrawal of the fractional currency led to some severe runs in consequence of an impression among the peasants, by whom the notes were principally held, that they would be valueless when the Act came into force.

Public officers were permitted to become partners in banks. It was enacted that Bank of England notes were not a legal tender in Ireland, and that directors of the Bank of Ireland were not to be required to take any other oaths than the oath of allegiance, the oath of qualification by the possession of stock, and the oath of fidelity.

The Act also required that the banks should return to the Stamp Office, in January of each year, a list of the partners or shareholders; and the powers and privileges of suing and being sued by their public officers were given to them.

The interest on advances by the Bank of Ireland to the Government was reduced to 3½ per cent. per annum,* and the management of the public debt was to be conducted free of charge.

Under this Act the Bank of Ireland lost the last of its remaining privileges. Although a chartered bank, and the repository of the Government account, its position differs from that of the Bank of England, as it enters into active competition with the banks of the country, and since 1864 has allowed interest on deposits. Its notes are not legal tender except in the payment of revenue.†

The authorised issues were fixed as follows:—

Bank of Ireland	£3,738,428
Belfast Banking Company ...	281,611
National Bank	852,269
Northern Banking Company ...	243,440
Provincial Bank of Ireland ...	927,667
Ulster Banking Company ...	311,079
	£6,354,494

* Further reduced in 1865 to 3 per cent.

† Evidence of Mr. P. Du Bedat before the House of Commons' Committee on Banks of Issue, 1875.

No alteration has since been made in them, except as regards the issues of the National Bank. These were, in 1845:—

Dublin	£761,757
Carrick-on-Suir	24,084
Clonmel	66,428
and they are now returned as	£852,269

It was at first contended that the Act had operated unfavourably, as the banks had no inducement to increase their circulation, and accordingly had withdrawn accommodation from various parts of the country. As a matter of fact, however, in the year following the passing of the Act, both the Note circulation and the total Deposits in Joint Stock Banks shewed considerable expansion. The average circulation in 1845 was £6,949,000, and in 1846 £7,266,000. In 1847 the figures dropped to £6,009,000, and in 1848 to £4,829,000, but this decline can be easily traced to the concurrent decrease in the population which had set in, as the result of the great potato famine of 1847. An exactly similar movement took place in the total deposits of Joint Stock Banks. In 1845 they amounted to £8,031,000 and they increased to £8,442,000 in 1846, falling in 1847 to £6,493,000.

The law relating to the payment of notes in Ireland is materially different from that of either England or Scotland. The notes of the Bank of England are payable either in London, or at the branch where issued. The notes of the Scotch banks are payable at the head offices only; but in Ireland the banks are compelled to pay their notes at the place of issue, and in practice it is their custom to pay them wherever they are presented. The banks are, therefore, obliged to hold sufficient gold at every branch to meet any notes that may be presented there. Previously to 1829, the Bank of Ireland was an exception in this respect, their notes, issued at Cork and elsewhere, being payable in Dublin only, and the effect of this being that during a run at Cork on the other banks, the notes of those banks were selling at a premium in exchange for Bank of Ireland notes on account of the holders being able to obtain gold for the one and not for the other. To place the Bank of Ireland on an equality with other issuing institutions, the Act, 9 Geo. IV., c. 81, was passed for the purpose of making all notes payable at the places where issued.

The result of this enactment is that the Irish banks are very large holders of specie. For the purpose of establishing a circulation which would be issuable at any point, in compliance with the requirement of the Act, the names of all the branches are specified upon the notes, so that a note issued at one branch is payable at all the others. Mr. E. J. Mills, then manager of the National Bank, in his evidence before the Select Committee of the House of Commons in 1875, said : " We are the largest specie holders in the Kingdom next to the Bank of England. We hold more gold and silver than any other bank in the United Kingdom next to the Bank of England. We hold £941,000 in specie."

For some time, considerable doubt existed as to whether Bank of England notes were a legal tender in Ireland. The Act (3 and 4 Wm. IV., c. 98, s. 6) of the Imperial Parliament, directed that a tender of a note of the Bank of England, expressed to be payable to bearer on demand, should be a legal tender for sums above £5, so long as the Bank of England should continue to pay its notes in legal coin, and as there were no words in the clause limiting its operation to England, it was contended that Bank of England notes were a legal tender in Ireland. The opinions of the most eminent counsel were obtained on the question, but there was no agreement among them, some deciding that the Act applied to Ireland, and others asserting that it did not. The Bank of Ireland also insisted that the notes were not legal tender. The cost and inconvenience of drawing gold from the Bank of England, which was often not required, to meet the case of temporary runs, and the want of some form of legal tender which would economise the use of gold coin, would have made the operation of the Act beneficial, though on the other hand, the absence of any establishment of the Bank of England, in Ireland, at which the notes could be exchanged for gold, would have rendered them inconvertible, and, consequently, depreciated their value ; but the doubts existing on the subject deterred any experiment being made. These doubts were, however, removed by the Act, 8 and 9 Vic., c. 37, enacting that notes of the Bank of England were not to be considered legal tender in Ireland.

CHAPTER XII.

SAVINGS BANKS AND LOAN FUNDS.

Origin of Trustee Savings Banks—Extension of the system to Ireland—Legislation—Rates of interest allowed—Losses by fraud—Investigation as to the failure of the Tralee Bank—Offer of the National Bank in 1848 to receive deposits of ten shillings—Institution of Post Office Savings Banks—Private hoarding—Statistics—Runs on Savings banks—Pawnbrokers in Ireland—Monts de Piété—Practice of pawning Bank notes and money—Charitable Loan Funds—Origin—Rates of interest charged—Progress of the Loan Funds—Comparative operation 1838–1888.

THE institution of Savings Banks in the United Kingdom, dates only from the beginning of the present century. Up to that time the privilege of "keeping a banker," however inadequate the facilities he may have been able to afford, was confined to the moneyed classes, and the desirability of extending the advantages of banking so as to bring them within reach of the poorer people, does not seem to have been apparent to legislators or social reformers. The idea of founding savings banks on a partially self-supporting basis, was first mooted in 1807, by Mr. S. Whitbread, when on the introduction of a Poor-Law Amendment Bill, he drew the attention of Parliament to the absence of any means by which the small savings of the poorer classes could be secured and the practice of thrift encouraged. Subsequently and principally through the influence of the clergy, some banks of this class were started in England and Scotland, but the progress made was at first slow, and did not extend to Ireland until 1815, when a savings bank was opened at Stillorgan, another being established in Belfast in the following year.

In 1817 the number of banks had so far increased as to justify the interference of the legislature, and an Act was passed providing that the moneys were to be paid over by the Trustees to the Commissioners for the reduction of the National Debt to be by them invested in 3 per cent. Bank Annuities, the Government paying the Trustees interest at the rate of £4 11*s.* 3*d.* per annum. Such a high rate of interest, however, was found to attract depositors other than those for whom the benefits of the banks were intended, and this led to a new Act being passed in 1824, limiting the amount to be deposited by any one person. The Government allowance of interest was reduced in 1828 to £3 16*s.* 0½*d.* per cent. and again in 1844 to the present rate of £3 5*s.* per cent. per annum.

But the wisdom of Parliament could not altogether prevent losses occasioned by fraud on the part of the trustees or their officials, and many painful instances of this kind occurred. In 1848, a wave of misfortune seems to have broken over the Irish Depositors. The Secretary of the Tralee Savings Bank absconded with £34,000 out of the total funds amounting to only £36,000*; the Cuffe Street Dublin bank suspended payment with liabilities of £50,000 and assets of £87; at Killarney there was a deficiency of about £36,000, and the Kerry and Bandon Banks also closed their doors owing to frauds on the part of the officials. These misfortunes were the means of an Act being passed in September, 1848, applying only to Ireland, regulating the liability of Trustees and providing for the appointment of Auditors.

Previously to the passing of this Act, Mr. John Tidd Pratt was appointed by the Government to conduct an investigation into the circumstances connected with the failure of the Tralee Bank. In his report he refers to the abuse of the institution by the depositors as well as the neglect and default of the managers. The provisions of the Act of 1828 limiting the amount of deposits to £30 in any one year, or £150 in all, had been entirely ignored. Claims were made by single

* The balance of £2,000 was standing at the credit of the Trustees with the Commissioners for the reduction of the National Debt. In 1876, (28 years after the failure) at the suggestion of Sir Stafford Northcote, then Chancellor of the Exchequer, an Act of Parliament was passed enabling the amount to be distributed without expense, and in the judgment of the arbitrators appointed under the Act, without legal proof, among the persons entitled thereto, or their representatives.

individuals for sums of £1,100, £850 and £620, etc. In one instance a deposit had been made in one day of £400, on account of an hospital, another of £483 in aid of a fund for building a chapel, and the Irish Productive Loan Fund had been allowed to invest a sum of more than £5,000 which was afterwards withdrawn. Several parties who were inmates of the workhouse, as well as recipients of the late relief fund appeared as claimants, and three persons who were in prison as debtors, came in the custody of the gaoler to claim deposits. The majority of the depositors, though to all appearances in the greatest destitution, had invested their money in order to avoid paying their rents or other legal claims upon them, and in numerous instances were living upon charity, or were the recipients of indoor or outdoor relief. The Inspector added that the investigation was rendered more painful by the almost utter disregard of truth, and the attempts at fraud, falsehood, and subornation of perjury which were made by the claimants.

It is worthy of note that in 1848, in consequence of the want of confidence engendered in the savings bank system, the National Bank offered to receive deposits of sums of ten shillings and upwards, at any of their branches, at the current rate of interest. Bankers have generally resisted any extension in the direction of Government banking as an interference with their interests, and this is probably the only instance of a bank entering into competition with what was practically a Government Department.

In 1861 the Post Office Savings Bank Act was passed, and the machinery of the Post Office with its absolute security and the facility it afforded of lodging or withdrawing money, was thus made available for the purposes of the people's bank. It will, however, be remarked on reference to the subjoined table that while the deposits in the Irish Post Office Savings Banks show great progress, the total deposits in Trustee Banks, although exhibiting some fluctuation, have not materially declined.

These figures may be taken to indicate an increase of means, and of the practice of thrift among the poorer classes, although, probably, a portion of the advance may be due to the diversion to the Post Office Savings Banks, of private hoards previously accumulated. There is no doubt that the failures of Trustee Banks just alluded to would create considerable distrust in the minds of depositors and encourage the practice of hoarding.

The following table* shows the deposits in Irish Post Office and Trustee Savings Banks stated separately and together, since 1861 :—

Date.	Post Office Savings Banks.	Trustee Savings Banks.	Total.
	£	£	£
1861, 31st December.	Not established.	2,153,000	2,153,000
1862, "	79,000	2,088,000	2,167,000
1863, "	144,000	2,072,000	2,216,000
1864, "	177,000	1,973,000	2,150,000
1865, "	207,000	1,837,000	2,044,000
1866, "	221,000	1,540,000	1,761,000
1867, "	260,000	1,633,000	1,893,000
1868, "	356,000	1,814,000	2,170,000
1869, "	458,000	1,975,000	2,433,000
1870, "	583,000	2,055,000	2,638,000
1871, "	687,000	2,208,000	2,895,000
1872, "	759,000	1,964,000	2,723,000
1873, "	764,000	2,075,000	2,839,000
1874, "	819,000	2,092,000	2,911,000
1875, "	888,000	2,044,000	2,932,000
1876, "	981,000	2,153,000	3,134,000
1877, "	1,084,000	2,220,000	3,304,000
1878, "	1,121,000	2,160,000	3,281,000
1879, "	1,181,000	2,098,000	3,279,000
1880, "	1,310,000	2,079,000	3,389,000
1881, "	1,513,000	2,042,000	3,555,000
1882, "	1,718,000	2,078,000	3,796,000
1883, "	1,834,000	2,060,000	3,894,000
1884, "	1,990,000	2,097,000	4,087,000
1885, "	2,202,000	1,981,000	4,183,000
1886, "	2,444,000	2,007,000	4,451,000
1887, "	2,932,000	2,043,000	4,975,000
1888, "	3,239,000	2,029,000	5,268,000

* These figures are taken from the "Report on certain Statistics of Banking in Ireland, &c.," by Thomas W. Grimshaw, Esq., Registrar General.

At various periods in their history the Trustee Savings banks have had to contend with runs and panics. In 1853 a run which originated in Cork and spread to Dublin was traced to the circumstance that the Cork Savings Bank had been closed for the purpose of making some alteration in the office arrangements, and this was taken by the depositors to mean that payment had been suspended.

But while thrift was fostered, the borrowing proclivities of the poor were not lost sight of. From a paper read before the British Association by Professor Hancock in 1849, it appears that there were then 447 pawnbrokers in Ireland lending about £2,000,000 at rates of interest varying from 53 to 85 per cent. per annum, and that these usurious rates were not, under the circumstances, excessive, had been proved by the failure of the *Monts de Piété*, established for the purpose of lending on pawns on more favourable terms than pawnbrokers. In 1841 there were eight of these institutions in Ireland, and in seven the operations resulted in a loss of £5,348 3*s.* 4*d.*, while in the remaining one, the profit amounted to only £8 8*s.* 5*d.*

The following extract from a letter which appeared in the *Times* in October, 1845, exemplifies the peculiar ideas of the people in regard to money.

"In Galway I was assured that so little do the people know of the value of money that they are constantly in the habit of pawning it. I was so incredulous of this, that the gentleman who informed me invited me to go with him to any pawnbroker to assure myself of the fact, and I went with him and another gentleman to a pawnbroker's shop kept by Mr. Murray, in Galway. On asking the question, the shopman said it was quite a common thing to have money pawned, and he produced a drawer containing:—

"A £10 Bank of Ireland note, pawned six months ago for 10*s*.
"A 30*s*. National Bank note. ,, ,, 10*s*.
"A 30*s*. Bank of Ireland note ,, ,, 1*s*.
"A 20*s*. Provincial Bank note ,, ,, 6*s*.

"and a guinea in gold, of the reign of George III., pawned for 15*s*. two months ago. The £10 note would produce 6*s*. 6*d*. interest in the year if put into the savings bank, whilst the owner, who pledged it for 10*s*., will have to pay 2*s*. 6*d*. a year for the 10*s*. and lose the interest on his £10; in other words, he will pay 90 per cent., through ignorance, for the use of 10*s*. which he might have had for nothing. Mr. Murray told me that often money was sold as a forfeited pledge; that a man would pawn a guinea for 15*s*., keep it in pledge till the interest amounted to 3*s*. or 4*s*., and then refuse to redeem it."

The system of "Charitable Loan Funds," established for the purpose of enabling industrious persons of the working classes to obtain advances of small amounts repayable by easy instalments, is peculiar to Ireland. In the year 1836, an Act* was passed authorising the formation of these Loan Funds, under the control of a Central Board in Dublin, and conferring on them the privilege of lending sums not exceeding £10, repayable in twenty instalments in as many weeks, at a charge not exceeding sixpence for each pound, equal to 13½ per cent. per annum, besides fines, the capital being raised by debentures at a rate of interest, not exceeding six per cent. per annum. By an Act passed in 1843,† the rate of interest allowed to be charged was reduced to fourpence in the pound, or 9½ per cent. The Loan Funds were authorised to proceed before the magistrates at Petty Sessions for the summary recovery of debts; no business was to be transacted at Hotels or Public Houses, the borrower was not to make any gratuity to the clerks or officers of the Funds and a proportion of the net profits was to be applied to charitable purposes. In 1842 there were 300 of these Funds in existence with outstanding loans amounting to £1,691,871, and up to 1845, when the total loans increased to £1,857,457, the figures were steadily progressive. In 1847 there was a sudden decline to £863,647, and it will be seen from the subjoined table exhibiting the state of the Loan Funds during the last fifty years, that the total amount of loans current was, in 1888, only £480,928. In 1848, the total extinction of the system seemed imminent. Many of the Societies were winding up their affairs, and the Trustees of the Lurgan Fund announced in their Report, dated February, 1848, that after ten years' experience, and the most careful enquiries they had arrived at the conclusion that the Charitable Loan system was productive of more evil than good. So lately, however, as the year 1888, the Loan Fund Board stated that they would not fail in their efforts to encourage the extension of a system which has invariably been found useful to many classes of people."

---

* 6 and 7 William IV., c. 55.

† 6 and 7 Victoria, c. 91.

The following table* shows the comparative operation of the Loan Funds at intervals of ten years :—

Year.	No. of Funds.	Capital.	Circulation.	Fines.	Gross Profit.	Net Profit.	Expended in Charity.	Total Number of Loans Granted.
		£	£	£	£	£	£	
1838	50	58,135	180,525	2,013	not stated.	2,547	597	148,528
1848	177	217,119	717,865	4,646	20,132	2,528	999	190,407
1858	111	237,728	930,170	4,878	26,550	7,459	2,183	200,200
1868	90	156,828	581,437	3,481	17,002	3,386	1,671	128,074
1878	81	142,034	491,863	4,112	15,449	2,396	1,307	98,838
1888	85	165,030	480,928	4,900	17,735	3,036	752	81,920

* Kindly furnished by Mr. A. G. Nicolls, Secretary to the Loan Fund Board of Ireland.

CHAPTER XIII.

STATISTICS.

Progress compared with England and Scotland—Population—Deposits, and average deposits per head 1840–1888—Remarks on the Table—Movements of banking capital, 1846–1888—Bank note circulation, 1844–1888—Average circulation, per head of population, in selected years.

IN conclusion, the progress of banking, from a statistical point of view, has to be considered. The figures presented in the accompanying tables do not exhibit the rapid expansion which is to be observed in statistics relating to banking in England or Scotland, but taken in conjunction with the decreasing population, the result is much more favourable to Ireland.

In the following table, the population and deposits in Joint Stock Banks, are given side by side with the banking deposits, per head, of the population. It will be seen that the average, per head, has increased from 13*s.* 8*d.*, in 1840, to £6 9*s.* 8*d.* in 1888.

DEPOSITS IN IRISH JOINT STOCK BANKS, 1840-1888.

Year.	Population.	Total Deposits and Cash Balances in Joint Stock Banks.	Increase or Decrease + or —	Banking Deposits per head of Population.
		£		£ s. d.
1840	8,155,521	5,567,851	...	0 13 8
1841	8,199,853	6,022,573	+ 454,722	0 14 8
1842	8,220,926	6,416,795	+ 394,222	0 15 7
1843	8,239,832	6,965,681	+ 548,866	0 16 11
1844	8,276,627	7,601,421	+ 635,740	0 18 4
1845	8,295,061	8,031,044	+ 429,623	0 19 4

Year.	Population.	Total Deposits and Cash Balances in Joint Stock Banks.	Increase or Decrease + or —	Banking Deposits per head of Population.
		£		£ s. d.
1846	8,287,848	8,442,133	+ 411,089	1 0 4
1847	8,025,274	6,493,124	— 1,949,009	0 16 2
1848	7,639,800	7,071,122	+ 577,998	0 18 6
1849	7,256,314	7,469,675	+ 398,553	1 0 7
1850	6,877,549	8,268,838	+ 799,163	1 4 1
1851	6,514,473	8,263,091	— 5,747	1 5 4
1852	6,336,889	10,773,324	+ 2,510,233	1 14 0
1853	6,198,984	10,915,022	+ 141,708	1 15 3
1854	6,083,183	11,665,739	+ 750,717	1 18 4
1855	6,014,665	12,285,822	+ 620,083	2 0 10
1856	5,972,851	13,753,149	+ 1,467,327	2 6 1
1857	5,919,454	13,113,136	— 640,013	2 4 4
1858	5,890,814	15,131,252	+ 2,018,116	2 11 4
1859	5,861,711	16,042,140	+ 910,888	2 14 9
1860	5,820,960	15,609,237	— 432,903	2 13 7
1861	5,788,415	15,005,065	— 604,172	2 11 10
1862	5,775,588	14,388,725	— 616,340	2 9 10
1863	5,718,235	12,967,000	— 1,421,725	2 5 4
1864	5,640,527	15,623,000	+ 2,656,000	2 15 5
1865	5,594,589	18,619,000	+ 2,996,000	3 6 7
1866	5,522,942	20,957,000	+ 2,338,000	3 15 11
1867	5,486,509	21,794,000	+ 837,000	3 19 5
1868	5,465,914	22,164,000	+ 370,000	4 1 4
1869	5,449,094	22,673,000	+ 509,000	4 3 3
1870	5,418,512	24,366,000	+ 1,693,000	4 9 11
1871	5,398,179	27,348,000	+ 2,982,000	5 1 4

Year.	Population.	Total Deposits and Cash Balances in Joint Stock Banks.	Increase or Decrease + or —	Banking Deposits per head of Population.
				£ s. d.
1872	5,372,890	28,732,000	+ 1,384,000	5 6 11
1873	5,327,938	29,210,000	+ 478,000	5 9 8
1874	5,298,979	31,734,000	+ 2,524,000	5 19 10
1875	5,278,629	33,519,000	+ 1,785,000	6 7 0
1876	5,277,544	34,240,000	+ 721,000	6 9 9
1877	5,286,380	33,050,000	— 1,190,000	6 5 0
1878	5,282,246	31,534,000	— 1,516,000	5 19 5
1879	5,265,625	30,541,000	— 993,000	5 16 0
1880	5,202,648	29,746,000	— 795,000	5 14 4
1881	5,144,983	30,161,000	+ 415,000	5 17 3
1882	5,097,853	32,746,000	+ 2,585,000	6 8 6
1883	5,015,282	31,340,000	— 1,406,000	6 5 0
1884	4,962,570	30,627,000	— 713,000	6 3 4
1885	4,924,342	29,370,000	— 1,257,000	5 19 4
1886	4,889,430	30,172,000	+ 802,000	6 3 4
1887	4,837,352	29,771,000	— 401,000	6 3 1
1888	4,777,545	30,979,000	+ 1,208,000	6 9 8

The Population returns are taken from the official estimates. The deposits and cash balances, up to 1862, are from Dr. Neilson Hancock's "Report on the supposed progressive decline of Irish Prosperity," and after 1862 from the Report of the Registrar-General of Ireland.

The above table embraces a period of forty-eight years, in thirty-three of which, the total deposits in joint stock banks have shewn an increase, while in fifteen there has been a retrogression. The progress was steady until 1847, the year of the great potato famine, when a fall of £1,949,000 was sustained, equal to 23 per cent. By 1850 this fall had been nearly recovered. In 1851 there was a slight diminution in the total, equal to about 0·07 per cent., but the figures again progressed until 1857, when, as the effect of the monetary and commercial crisis of that year, there was again a sharp fall, equal to 4 per cent. In 1858–1859 considerable expansion took place, but the four unfavourable years 1860–1863 resulted in a fall of 10 per cent. In 1864 this loss was recovered, and by 1876 the figures had nearly doubled. Since 1877 the decline has been continuous, except in the four years 1881, 1882, 1886 and 1888.

Since 1846 the following movements of banking capital have taken place.*

Years.	Paid-up.	Years.	Paid-up.
	£		£
1846–50	4,934,000	1869–70	6,392,000
1851–53	4,955,000	1871–2	6,547,000
1854	4,892,000	1873	6,672,000
1855	4,932,000	1874–5	6,759,000
1856	4,911,000	1876–9	6,809,000
1857	4,961,000	1880–1	6,954,000
1858–61	4,957,000	1882	6,984,000
1862	5,178,000	1883	7,367,000
1863	5,146,000	1884	7,204,000
1864	6,104,000	1885	6,679,000
1865	5,668,000	1886	6,872,000
1866	6,278,000	1887	6,879,000
1867	6,354,000	1888	6,932,843
1868	6,373,000		

Between 1851 and 1861 there was some fluctuation in the total figures, but from 1861 to 1885 the progress was steady. In the latter year a fall of £525,000 took place, being the amount of the paid-up capital of the Munster Bank, which had stopped payment. Since 1885 some progress has again been made, and in 1888 the total was £6,932,843.

* With the exception of the years 1865 and 1888, the figures are extracted from Dr. T. W. Grimshaw's address to the Statistical and Social Enquiry Society of Ireland. Session 1888–1889.

It is to be remarked that the liability of shareholders in Irish banks amounts to nearly 50 per cent. of the total liabilities of the banks to the public.

The following table* shews the bank note circulation from 1844 to 1888 :—

Year.	Amount.	Year.	Amount.
	£		£
1844	5,940,000	1867	5,811,000
1845	6,949,000	1868	6,181,000
1846	7,266,000	1869	6,608,000
1847	6,009,000	1870	6,880,000
1848	4,829,000	1871	7,544,000
1849	4,310,000	1872	7,674,000
1850	4,512,000	1873	7,077,000
1851	4,463,000	1874	6,772,000
1852	4,818,000	1875	7,064,000
1853	5,650,000	1876	7,499,000
1854	6,296,000	1877	7,399,000
1855	6,362,000	1878	6,984,000
1856	6,652,000	1879	6,065,000
1857	6,822,000	1880	6,127,000
1858	6,183,000	1881	6,587,000
1859	6,870,000	1882	7,297,000
1860	6,840,000	1883	7,124,000
1861	6,266,000	1884	6,513,000
1862	5,638,000	1885	6,062,000
1863	5,405,000	1886	6,018,000
1864	5,607,000	1887	5,885,000
1865	5,987,000	1888	6,057,000
1866	5,884,000		

* The figures for 1844–1879 are from Mr. John Biddulph Martin's tables, and for 1880–1888, from the returns published in the *Dublin Gazette*.

The following table shews the average bank note circulation per head of the population in selected years :—

000 omitted.

Year.	Population.	Bank Note Circulation.	Average per head of Population. Ireland.	United Kingdom.
			£ *s.* *d.*	£ *s.* *d.*
1848	7,640	4,829	0 12 8	1 3 3
1858	5,891	6,183	1 1 0	1 5 7
1868	5,466	6,181	1 2 7	1 5 11
1878	5,282	6,894	1 6 5	1 6 8
1888	4,778	6,057	1 5 4	1 0 9

It will be seen that the average circulation in 1888 shews a decline, compared with 1878, of 1*s.* 1*d.* per head, but the average circulation in the United Kingdom has declined 5*s.* 11*d.* per head during the same period.

The foregoing statistics, indicating the course and growth of the country's trade, and reflecting the expansion which has taken place in its material wealth, certainly afford some refutation of the alleged decline in Irish prosperity and industries. No less do they demonstrate the important part which banking has taken in the economic progress which the figures reveal.

APPENDIX.

The Irish Banking Act, 8 and 9 Victoria, c. 37.

Copy of the Charter of the Corporation of the Governor and Company of the Bank of Ireland.

List of the Original Governors, Directors and Subscribers to the Bank of Ireland, with their several Subscriptions affixed in the order they subscribed.

Rules, Orders and Bye-laws for the good government of the Corporation of the Governor and Company of the Bank of Ireland.

THE IRISH BANKING ACT.

8 and 9 Victoria, Cap. 37.

CAP. XXXVII.

An Act to regulate the Issue of Bank Notes in *Ireland*, and to regulate the Repayment of certain Sums advanced by the Governor and Company of the Bank of *Ireland* for the Public Service.

[21st *July*, 1845.]

Whereas by an Act passed in the Parliament of *Ireland* in the Twenty-first and Twenty-second Years of the Reign of His Majesty King *George* the Third,
21 & 22 G. 3. (I.) intituled *An Act for establishing a Bank by the Name of the Governors and Company of the Bank of* Ireland, it was amongst other things enacted, that from and after the passing of that Act it should not be lawful for any Body Politic or Corporate erected or to be erected, other than the Corporation thereby intended to be created and erected into a National Bank, or for any other Persons whatsoever united or to be united in Covenants or Partnership exceeding the Number of Six Persons, to borrow, owe, or take up any Sum or Sums of Money on their Bills or Notes payable at Demand, or at any less Time than Six Months from the borrowing thereof, under a Penalty or Forfeiture by such Persons, Bodies Politic or Corporate, of treble the Sum or Sums so to be borrowed or taken upon such Bill or Bills, Note or Notes, one Moiety thereof

to be paid to the Informer, and the other to the Use of His Majesty, His Heirs and Successors, to be recovered by Action of Debt, Bill, Plaint, or Information in any of His Majesty's Courts of Record at *Dublin:* And whereas, in pursuance of the Powers in the said Act of Parliament contained, a Charter of Incorporation was granted to certain Persons, by the Name of the Governor and Company of the Bank of *Ireland:* And whereas by an Act passed in the First and Second Years of the Reign of His Majesty King *George* the Fourth, intituled *An Act to establish an Agreement with the Governor and Company of the Bank of* Ireland *for advancing the Sum of Five hundred thousand Pounds* Irish *Currency, and to empower the said Governor and Company to enlarge the Capital Stock or Fund of the said Bank to Three million Pounds*, it was enacted, that it might be lawful for any Number of Persons in *Ireland* united or to be united in Society or Partnership, and residing and having their Establishments in Houses of Business at any Place not less than Fifty Miles distant from *Dublin*, to borrow, owe, or take up any Sum or Sums of Money on their Bills or Notes payable on Demand, and to make and issue such Notes or Bills accordingly, payable on Demand at any Place in *Ireland* exceeding the Distance of Fifty Miles from *Dublin*, all the Individuals composing such Societies or Partnerships being liable and responsible for the due Payment of such Bills or Notes; but nothing therein contained was to extend or be construed to extend to authorise any Persons exceeding Six in Number, or any Bodies Politic or Corporate, residing or having their Establishment or House of Business within the Distance of Fifty Miles from *Dublin*, to make or issue any Bill or Bills of Exchange, or any Promissory Note or Notes, contrary to the Provisions of the said in part recited Act of the Twenty-first and Twenty-second Years of the Reign of King *George* the Third: And whereas by another Act passed in the Sixth Year of the Reign of His Majesty King *George* the Fourth, intituled *An Act for the better Regulation of Copartnerships of certain Bankers in* Ireland, and by another Act passed in the First Year of the Reign of His late Majesty King *William* the Fourth, intituled *An Act to explain Two Acts of His present Majesty, for establishing an Agreement with the Governor and Company of the Bank of* Ireland *for advancing the Sum of Five hundred thousand Pounds* Irish *Currency, and for the better Regulation of Copartnerships of certain Bankers in* Ireland, such Copartnerships of Bankers established at Places beyond the Distance of Fifty Miles from *Dublin* were authorized to transact certain Matters of Business by Agents in *Dublin* or within the Distance of Fifty Miles thereof: And whereas the said Governor and Company at different Times advanced, for the Public Service, to His Majesty King *George* the Third, the several Sums of Six hundred thousand Pounds, Five hundred thousand Pounds, and One million two hundred and fifty thousand Pounds, late *Irish* Currency, and in respect thereof the said Governor and Company were entitled to certain Annuities payable at the Receipt of the Exchequer in *Dublin:* And whereas by an Act passed in the Forty-eighth Year of the Reign of His said Majesty King *George* the Third, intituled *An*

Act for further extending the Provisions of several Acts for establishing the Bank of Ireland, *and for empowering the Governor and Company of the said Bank to advance the Sum of One million two hundred and fifty thousand Pounds* Irish *Currency towards the Service of the Year One thousand eight hundred and eight*, it was amongst other things enacted, that at any Time after the First Day of *January* in the Year of our Lord One thousand eight hundred and thirty-seven, upon Twelve Months Notice, to be published in the *Dublin Gazette* by Order of the Lord Lieutenant or other Chief Governor or Governors of *Ireland*, the said Corporation of the Bank was to be dissolved; and upon repayment by Parliament to the said Governor and Company of the Bank of *Ireland*, or their Successors, of the said several Sums of Six hundred thousand Pounds, Five hundred thousand Pounds, and One million two hundred and fifty thousand Pounds, and also of all Arrears of the several Annuities payable in respect of the said Three several Capital Sums, if any such Arrear should then be due, or at any Time previous to the said First Day of *January* One thousand eight hundred and thirty-seven, upon like Repayment, by and with the Desire and Consent of the said Governor and Company, to be signified by them by their Petition in Writing sealed with their Common Seal, and addressed to the Lord Lieutenant or other Chief Governor or Governors of *Ireland* for the Time being, then and in such Case the said several Annuities should from and after the Expiration of Twelve Months after such Notice published, cease and determine, and the said Corporation should be dissolved: And whereas in pursuance of the said recited Act passed in the First and Second Years of the
1 & 2 G. 4. c. 72 Reign of His Majesty King *George* the Fourth, intituled *An Act to establish an Agreement with the Governor and Company of the Bank of* Ireland *for advancing the Sum of Five hundred thousand Pounds* Irish *Currency, and to empower the said Governor and Company to enlarge the Capital Stock or Fund of the said Bank to Three Millions*, the said Governor and Company of the Bank of *Ireland* advanced for the Public Service, to His Majesty King *George* the Fourth, the Sum of Five hundred thousand Pounds late *Irish* Currency, at Interest, making, with the said Three several Sums of Six hundred thousand Pounds, Five hundred thousand Pounds, and One million two hundred and fifty thousand Pounds, late *Irish* Currency, previously advanced, the Sum of Two million eight hundred and fifty thousand Pounds, equal to Two million six hundred and thirty thousand seven hundred and sixty-nine Pounds Four Shillings and Eight-pence Sterling Money of the United Kingdom of *Great Britain* and *Ireland*: And whereas by an Act passed in the Third and Fourth Years of the
3 & 4 Vict. c. 75. Reign of Her present Majesty, intituled *An Act to regulate the Repayment of certain Sums advanced by the Governor and Company of the Bank of* Ireland *for the Public Service*, it was amongst other things enacted, that from and after the passing of the said Act there should be paid and payable, but subject to the Condition of Redemption therein-after contained, at the Receipt of Her Majesty's Exchequer in *Dublin*, to the Governor and Company of the said Bank of *Ireland*, out of the Consolidated Fund of the United Kingdom of *Great*

Britain and *Ireland*, an Interest or Annuity of One hundred and fifteen thousand three hundred and eighty-four Pounds Twelve Shillings and Four-pence, Money of the United Kingdom, being a Sum equal to the several Annuities and Interest theretofore payable in respect of the Principal Money due to the said Governor and Company as aforesaid, by Two equal half-yearly Payments, without any Defalcation or Abatement, on the Fifth Day of *January* and the Fifth Day of *July* in each Year, the first Payment of the said Interest or Annuity to be made on the Fifth Day of *January* in the Year One thousand eight huudred and forty-one; and it was by the last-mentioned Act further provided, that the said last-mentioned Annuity should be redeemable at any Time after the First Day of *January* One thousand eight hundred and forty-one, on Six Months Notice to the said Governor and Company, and on Repayment to them of the said several Sums of Six hundred thousand Pounds, Five hundred thousand Pounds, One million two hundred and fifty thousand Pounds, and Five hundred thousand Pounds, late *Irish* Currency, together with all Arrears of the said Annuity of One hundred and fifteen thousand three hundred and eighty-four Pounds Twelve Shillings and Four-pence: And whereas the last-mentioned Annuity has, by Consent of the said Governor and Company, been reduced to an Annuity of Ninety-two thousand and seventy-six Pounds Eighteen Shillings and Five-pence of *British* Currency: And whereas it is expedient that the exclusive Privilege of Banking granted to the said Governor and Company by the said recited Act of the Parliament of *Ireland*, or by any other Act or Acts of Parliament now in force, should cease, but that the said Governor and Company should continue a Corporation, with full Power and Authority to carry on the Business of Bankers, subject to the Regulations herein-after contained; and the said Governor and Company of the Bank of *Ireland* have agreed to continue the Management in *Ireland* of so much of the Public Debt of the United Kingdom as shall for the Time being require to be transacted in *Ireland*, and of all Loans and other Creations of Stock which shall at any Time be made in *Ireland*, and of any Public Annuities for Lives or for Years which may be payable in *Ireland*, free of all Charge and Expence whatever for such Management, or for their Trouble in the Payment of the Interest of the said Public Debt or Annuities from Time to Time during the Continuance of the said Corporation under the Provisions of this Act; and it hath been further agreed that the said Governor and Company shall continue to receive the said Annuity of Ninety-two thousand and seventy-six Pounds Eighteen Shillings and Five-pence, being an annual Interest at and after the Rate of Three and a Half *per Centum per Annum*, for and in respect of the said Capital Sum of Two million six hundred and thirty thousand seven hundred and sixty-nine Pounds Four Shillings and Eight-pence, and that the Repayment of the last-mentioned Sum shall be postponed till the Expiration of Six Months after Notice to be given by the Commissioners of Her Majesty's Treasury of the United Kingdom of *Great Britain* and *Ireland* to the said Governor and Company of their Intention to pay off the same, or by the said

Governor and Company to the said Commissioners of Her Majesty's Treasury requiring Payment thereof, such Notice not to be given by either Party before the First Day of *January* One thousand eight hundred and fifty-five: And whereas by an Act passed in the Seventh and Eighth Years of the Reign of Her Majesty, intituled *An Act to regulate the Issue of Bank Notes, and for giving to the Governor and Company of the Bank of* England *certain Privileges for a limited Period*, it was enacted, that from and after the passing of that Act no Person, other than a Banker, who on the Sixth Day of *May* One thousand eight hundred and forty-four was lawfully issuing his own Bank Notes, should make or issue Bank Notes in any Part of the United Kingdom: And whereas it is expedient to regulate the Issue of Bank Notes by the said Governor and Company of the Bank of *Ireland*, and by such other Bankers as are now by Law authorized to issue Bank Notes in *Ireland*: Be it therefore enacted by the Queen's most Excellent Majesty, by and with the Advice and Consent of the Lords Spiritual and Temporal, and Commons, in this present Parliament assembled, and by the Authority of the same, That from and after the Sixth Day of *December* One thousand eight hundred and forty-five so much of the said recited Act of the Parliament of *Ireland* of the Twenty-first and Twenty-second Years of the Reign of His Majesty King *George* the Third as prohibits any Body Politic or Corporate erected or to be erected, other than the Governor and Company of the Bank of *Ireland*, or for any other Persons whatsoever united or to be united in Covenants or Partnership exceeding the Number of Six Persons, to borrow, owe, or take up any Sum or Sums of Money on their Bills or Notes payable at Demand, or at any less Time than Six Months from the borrowing thereof, shall be and the same is hereby repealed; and that from and after the said Sixth Day of *December* One thousand eight hundred and forty-five it shall and may be lawful for any Persons exceeding Six in Number united or to be united in Societies or Partnerships, or for any Bodies Politic or Corporate, to transact or carry on the Business of Bankers in *Ireland* at *Dublin*, and at every Place within Fifty Miles thereof, as freely as Persons exceeding Six in Number united as aforesaid may lawfully carry on the same Business at any Place in *Ireland* beyond the Distance of Fifty Miles from *Dublin*: Provided always, that every Member of any such Society, Partnership, Bodies Politic or Corporate, shall be liable and responsible for the due Payment of all the Debts and Liabilities of the Corporation or Copartnership of which such Person shall be a Member, any Agreement, Covenant, or Contract to the contrary notwithstanding.

II. And be it enacted, That from and after the passing of this Act the Repayment of the said Sum of Two million six hundred and thirty thousand seven hundred and sixty-nine Pounds Four Shillings and Eight-pence shall be and the same is hereby made chargeable upon the Consolidated Fund of the United Kingdom of *Great Britain* and *Ireland* until Parliament shall otherwise provide, and there shall be paid and payable, but subject to the Condition of Redemption herein-after contained, at the Receipt of Her Majesty's Exchequer in *Dublin*, to the Governor and Company of the said Bank of *Ireland*, out of the Consolidated Fund of the United Kingdom of *Great Britain* and *Ireland*, in respect of the said Capital Sum of Two million six hundred and thirty thousand seven hundred and sixty-nine Pounds Four Shillings and Eight-pence so now due by the Public to the said Governor and Company, the aforesaid Annuity of Ninety-two thousand and seventy-six Pounds Eighteen Shillings and Five-pence. being an Interest or Annuity at and after the Rate of Three Pounds Ten Shillings *per Centum per Annum*, in the now lawful Currency of the United Kingdom, by Two equal half-yearly Payments, without any Defalcation or Abatement, on the Fifth Day of *January* and the Fifth day of *July* in each Year.

III. And be it enacted, That from and after the passing of this Act the said Governor and Company of the Bank of *Ireland* shall from Time to Time and at all Times during the Continuance of their Charter, and until the said Corporation shall be dissolved pursuant to the Provisions of this Act, continue to manage and to pay all Interest, Annuities, and Dividends payable at the said Bank in respect of such Part of the Public Debt as shall for the Time being require to be transacted in *Ireland*, or in respect of any Fund or Stock created or to be created in consequence of any Public Loan, or funding of Exchequer Bills, or Conversion of Stock in *Ireland*, or of any Public Annuities, whether for Lives or for Years, without making any Charge to Her Majesty, Her Heirs or Successors, or to the Lord High Treasurer or the Commissioners of Her Majesty's Treasury, for their Trouble or Expence in so doing, any Law, Usage, or Custom to the contrary notwithstanding.

IV. And be it enacted, That at any Time after the First Day of *January* which will be in the Year of our Lord One thousand eight hundred and fifty-five, upon Twelve Months Notice, to be published in the *Dublin Gazette* by Order of the Lord Lieutenant or other Chief Governor or Governors of *Ireland*, that the said Corporation of the Bank is to be dissolved, and upon Repayment by Parliament to the said Governor and Company of the Bank of *Ireland*, or their Successors, of the said sum of Two million six hundred and thirty thousand seven hundred and sixty-nine Pounds Four Shillings and Eight-pence, together with all Arrears of Interest or Annuity due in respect thereof, then and in such Case the said Interest or Annuity shall from and after the Expiration of Twelve Months after such Notice published, cease and determine and the said Corporation shall be dissolved.

V. And whereas by an Act passed in the Parliament of *Ireland* in the Thirty-third Year of His late Majesty King *George* the Second, intituled *An Act for repealing an Act passed in this Kingdom in the Eighth Year of the Reign of King* George *the First, intituled 'An Act for the better securing the 'Payment of Bankers Notes, and for providing a more effectual Remedy for the 'Security and Payment of Debts due by Bankers,'* it was among other things enacted, that no Person who by reason of any Office, Employment, Deputation, or Clerkship was then or should at any Time thereafter be entrusted with the Receipt, Custody, or Payment of Public Money, or any Part of the Public Revenue of that kingdom, should, either singly or in Partnership, so long as such Person should continue in such office, Employment, Deputation, or Clerkship, follow the Trade or Business of a Banker, or by himself, or by any Person authorized by him, issue or give any Note or accountable Receipt as a Banker or in Partnership with any Banker, or for Profit or Reward discount any Promissory Note, or Foreign or Inland Bill of Exchange: And whereas it is expedient to repeal the said Enactment; be it therefore enacted, That from and after the passing of this Act so much of the last-mentioned Act as is herein recited shall be and the same is hereby repealed.

VI. And whereas by an Act passed in the Third and Fourth Years of the Reign of His late Majesty King *William* the Fourth, intituled *An Act for giving to the Corporation of the Governor and Company of the Bank of* England *certain Privileges for a limited Period, under certain Conditions*, it was enacted, that from and after the First Day of *August* One thousand eight hundred and thirty-four, unless and until Parliament should otherwise direct, a Tender of a Note or Notes of the Governor and Company of the Bank of *England* expressed to be payable to Bearer on Demand should be a legal Tender to the Amount expressed in such Note or Notes, and should be taken to be valid as a Tender to such Amount for all Sums above Five Pounds, on all Occasions on which any Tender of Money may be legally made, so long as the Bank of *England* should continue to pay on Demand their said Notes in legal Coin; provided always, that no such Note or Notes should be deemed a legal Tender of Payment by the Governor and Company of the Bank of *England*, or any Branch Bank of the said Governor and Company: And whereas Doubts have arisen as to the Extent of the said Enactment; for Removal whereof, be it enacted and declared, That nothing in the said last-recited Act contained shall extend or be construed to extend to make the Tender of a Note or Notes of the Governor and Company of the Bank of *England* a legal Tender in *Ireland*: Provided also, that nothing in this Act shall be construed to prohibit the Circulation in *Ireland* of the Notes of the Governor and Company of the Bank of *England* as heretofore.

VII. And be it enacted, That from and after the passing of this Act it shall not be necessary for any Governor, Deputy Governor, or Director of the said Bank, before acting in the said several Offices or Trusts, to make and subscribe the Declaration pursuant to the Act of Parliament passed in the Kingdom of *Ireland*, intituled *An Act to prevent the further Growth of Popery*, nor to take any other Oaths than the Oath of Allegiance, the Oath of Qualification by Possession of Stock, and the Oath of Fidelity to the Corporation prescribed in and by the Charter of Incorporation of the Governor and Company of the said Bank, and that it shall not be necessary for any Member of the said Corporation, before voting in any General Court, to make and subscribe the aforesaid Declaration, nor to take any other Oaths than the Oaths of Allegiance, the Oath of Qualification by the Possession of Stock, and the Oath of Fidelity to the said Corporation provided in the said Charter of Incorporation: Provided always, that in case any of the Persons called Quakers shall at any Time be chosen Governor, Deputy Governor, or Director, or shall be or become a Member of the said Corporation, it shall be sufficient for such Person or Persons to make his or their solemn Affirmation, to the Purport and Effect of the Oaths prescribed by the said Charter and by this Act to be taken by Governors, Deputy Governors, Directors, or Members respectively of the said Corporation.

VIII. And be it enacted, That every Banker claiming to be entitled to issue Bank Notes in *Ireland* shall, within One Month next after the passing of this Act, give Notice in Writing to the Commissioners of Stamps and Taxes, at their head Office in *London*, of such Claim, and of the Place and Name and Firm at and under which such Banker has issued such Notes in *Ireland* during the Year next preceding the First Day of *May* One thousand eight hundred and forty-five, and thereupon the said Commissioners shall ascertain if such Banker was on the Sixth Day of *May* One thousand eight hundred and forty-four, and from thence up to the First Day of *May* One thousand eight hundred and forty-five, carrying on the Business of a Banker, and lawfully issuing his own Bank Notes in *Ireland*, and if it shall so appear, then the said Commissioners shall proceed to ascertain the average Amount of the Bank Notes of such Banker which were in Circulation during the said Period of One Year preceding the First Day of *May* One thousand eight hundred and forty-five, according to the Returns made by such Banker in pursuance of the Act passed in the Fourth and Fifth Years of the Reign of Her present Majesty, intituled *An Act to make further Provisions relative to the Returns to be made by Banks of the Amount of their Notes in Circulation*, and the said Commissioners, or any Two of them, shall certify under their Hands to such Banker the average Amount, when so ascertained as aforesaid, omitting the Fractions of a Pound, if any; and it shall be lawful for every such Banker to continue to issue his own Bank Notes after the Sixth Day of *December* One thousand eight hundred and forty-five, to the Extent of the Amount so certified, and of the Amount of the Gold and Silver Coin held by such Banker, in the Proportion and Manner herein-after mentioned, but not to any further Extent; and from and after the Sixth Day of *December* One thousand eight hundred and forty-five it shall not be lawful for any Banker to make or issue Bank Notes in *Ireland*, save and except only such Bankers as shall have obtained such Certificate from the Commissioners of Stamps and Taxes.

IX. Provided always, and be it enacted, That if it shall be made to appear to the Commissioners of Stamps and Taxes that any Two or more Banks have, by written Contract or Agreement (which Contract or Agreement shall be produced to the said Commissioners), become united within the Year next preceding such First Day of *May* One thousand eight hundred and forty-five, it shall be lawful for the said Commissioners to ascertain the average Amount of the Notes of each such Bank in the Manner herein-before directed, and to certify a Sum equal to the average Amount of the Notes of the Two or more Banks so united as the Amount which the united Bank shall thereafter be authorized to issue, subject to the Regulations of this Act.

X. And be it enacted, That the Commissioners of Stamps and Taxes shall, at the Time of certifying to any Banker such Particulars as they are herein-before required to certify, also publish a Duplicate of their Certificate thereof in the next succeeding *Dublin Gazette* in which the same may be conveniently inserted; and the Gazette in which such Publication shall be made shall be conclusive Evidence in all Courts whatsoever of the Amount of Bank Notes which the Banker named in such Certificate or Duplicate is by Law authorized to issue and to have in Circulation as aforesaid, exclusive of an Amount equal to the monthly average Amount of the Gold and Silver Coin held by such Banker as herein provided.

XI. And be it enacted, That in case it shall be made to appear to the Commissioners of Stamps and Taxes at any Time hereafter that any Two or more Banks have, by written Contract or Agreement (which Contract or Agreement shall be produced to the said Commissioners), become united subsequently to the passing of this Act, it shall be lawful to the said Commissioners, upon the Application of such united Bank, to certify, in manner herein-before mentioned, the Aggregate of the Amount of Bank Notes which such separate Banks were previously authorised to issue under the separate Certificates previously delivered to them, and so from Time to Time; and every such Certificate shall be published in manner herein-before directed; and from and after such Publication the Amount therein stated shall be and be deemed to be the Limit of the Amount of Bank Notes which such united Bank may have in Circulation, exclusive of an Amount equal to the monthly average Amount of the Gold and Silver Coin held by such Banker as herein provided.

XII. And be it enacted, That it shall be lawful for any Banker in *Ireland* who under the Provisions of this Act is entitled to issue Bank Notes to contract and agree with the Governor and Company of the Bank of *Ireland*, by an Agreement in Writing, for the Relinquishment of the Privilege of issuing such Notes in favour of the said Governor and Company, and in each such Case a Copy of such Agreement shall be transmitted to the Commissioners of Stamps and Taxes; and the said Commissioners shall thereupon certify, in manner herein-before mentioned, the Aggregate of the Amount of Bank Notes which the Bank of *Ireland* and the Banker with whom such Agreement shall have been made were previously authorised to issue under the separate Certificates previously delivered to them; and every such Certificate shall be published in manner herein-before directed; and from and after such Publication the Amount therein stated shall be the Limit of the Amount of Bank Notes which the Governor and Company of the Bank of *Ireland* may have in Circulation, exclusive of an Amount equal to the Amount of the Gold and Silver Coin held by the Bank of *Ireland* as herein provided.

XIII. And be it enacted, That it shall not be lawful for any Banker who shall have so agreed to relinquish the Privilege of issuing Bank Notes at any Time thereafter to issue any such Notes.

XIV. And be it enacted, That from and after the Sixth Day of *December* One thousand eight hundred and forty-five it shall not be lawful for any Banker in *Ireland* to have in Circulation, upon the Average of a Period of Four Weeks, to be ascertained as herein-after mentioned, a greater Amount of Notes than an Amount composed of the Sums certified by the Commissioners of Stamps and Taxes as aforesaid, and the monthly average amount of Gold and Silver Coin held by such Banker during the same Period of Four Weeks, to be ascertained in manner herein-after mentioned.

XV. And be it enacted, That all Bank Notes to be issued or re-issued in *Ireland* after the Sixth Day of *December* One Thousand eight hundred and forty-five shall be expressed to be for Payment of a Sum in Pounds Sterling, without any fractional Parts of a Pound; and if any Banker in *Ireland* shall from and after that Day make, sign, issue, or re-issue any Bank Note for the fractional Part of a Pound Sterling, or for any Sum together with the fractional Part of a Pound Sterling, every such Banker so making, signing, issuing, or re-issuing any such Note as aforesaid shall for each Note so made, signed, issued, or re-issued forfeit or pay the Sum of Twenty Pounds.

XVI. And be it enacted, That every Banker who after the Sixth Day of *December* One thousand eight hundred and forty-five shall issue Bank Notes in *Ireland* shall, on some one Day in every Week after the Thirteenth Day of *December* One thousand eight hundred and forty-five (such Day to be fixed by the Commissioners of Stamps and Taxes), transmit to the said Commissioners a just and true account of the Amount of Bank Notes of such Banker in Circulation at the Close of the Business on the next preceding *Saturday*, distinguishing the Notes of Five Pounds and upwards, and the Notes below Five Pounds, and also an Account of the total Amount of Gold and Silver Coin held by such Banker at each of the head Offices or principal Places of Issue in *Ireland* of such Banker at the close of Business on each Day of the Week ending on that *Saturday*, and also an Account of the total Amount of Gold and Silver Coin in *Ireland* held by such Banker at the Close of Business on that Day; and on completing the first Period of Four Weeks, and so on completing each successive Period of Four Weeks, every such Banker shall annex to such Account the average Amount of Bank Notes of such Banker in Circulation during the said Four Weeks, distinguishing the Bank Notes of Five Pounds and upwards, and the Notes below Five Pounds, and the average Amount of Gold and Silver Coin respectively held by such Banker at each of the head Offices or principal places of Issue in *Ireland* of such Banker during the said Four Weeks, and also the Amount of Bank Notes which such Banker is, by the Certificate published as aforesaid, authorized to issue under the Provisions of this Act; and every such Account shall be verified by the Signature of such Banker or his Chief Cashier, or in the Case of a Company or Partnership by the Signature of the Chief Cashier or other Officer duly authorized by the Directors of such Company or Partnership, and shall be made in the Form to this Act annexed marked (A.); and if any such Banker shall neglect or refuse to render any such Account in the Form and at the Time required by this Act, or shall at any Time render a false account, such Banker shall forfeit the Sum of One hundred Pounds for every such Offence.

XVII. And be it enacted, That all Bank Notes shall be deemed to be in Circulation from the Time the same shall have been issued by any Banker, or any Servant or Agent of such Banker, until the same shall have been actually returned to such Banker, or some Servant or Agent of such Banker.

XVIII. And be it enacted, That from the Returns so made by each Banker to the Commissioners of Stamps and Taxes the said Commissioners shall, at the End of the first Period of Four Weeks after the said Sixth Day of *December* One thousand eight hundred and forty-five, and so at the End of each successive Period of Four Weeks, make out a general Return in the Form to this Act annexed marked (B.) of the monthly average Amount of Bank Notes in Circulation of each Banker in *Ireland* during the last preceding Four Weeks, and of the average Amount of all the Gold and Silver Coin held by such Banker during the same period, and certifying, under the Hand of any Officer of the said Commissioners duly authorized for that Purpose in the Case of each such Banker, whether such Banker has held the Amount of Coin required by Law during the period to which the said Return shall apply, and shall publish the same in the next succeeding *Dublin Gazette* in which the same can be conveniently inserted.

XIX. And be it enacted, That for the Purpose of ascertaining the monthly average Amount of Bank Notes of each Banker in Circulation, the Aggregate of the Amount of Bank Notes of each such Banker in Circulation at the Close of the Business on the *Saturday* in each Week during the first complete Period of Four Weeks next after the Sixth Day of *December* One thousand eight hundred and forty-five shall be divided by the Number of Weeks, and the Average so ascertained shall be deemed to be the Average of Bank Notes of each such Banker in Circulation during such period of Four Weeks, and so in each successive Period of Four Weeks; and the monthly average Amount of Gold and Silver Coin respectively held as aforesaid by such Banker shall be ascertained in like Manner from the Amount of Gold and Silver Coin held by such Banker at the head Offices or principal Places of Issue of such Banker in *Ireland*, as after mentioned, at the Close of Business on such Day in each Week; and the monthly average Amount of Bank Notes of each such Banker in Circulation during any such Period of Four Weeks is not to exceed a sum made up by adding the Amount certified by the Commissioners of Stamps and Taxes as aforesaid and the monthly average Amount of Gold and Silver Coin held by such Banker as aforesaid during the same Period.

XX. And be it enacted, That in taking account of the Coin held by any Banker in *Ireland* with respect to which Bank Notes to a further Extent than the Sum certified as aforesaid by the Commissioners of Stamps and Taxes may, under the Provisions of this Act, be made and issued, there shall be included only the Gold and Silver Coin held by such Banker at the several head Offices or principal Places of Issue in *Ireland* of such Banker, such head Offices or principal Places of Issue not exceeding Four in Number, of which not more than Two shall be situated in the same Province; and every Banker shall give Notice in Writing to the said Commissioners, on or before the Sixth Day of *December* next, of such head Offices or principal Places of Issue at which the Account of Gold and Silver Coin held by him is to be taken as aforesaid; and no Amount of Silver Coin exceeding One Fourth Part of the Gold Coin held by such Banker as aforesaid shall be taken into account, nor shall any Banker be authorized to make and Issue Bank Notes in *Ireland* on any Amount of Silver Coin held by such Banker exceeding the Proportion of One Fourth Part of the Gold Coin held by such Banker as aforesaid.

Commissioners of Stamps and Taxes empowered to cause the Books of Bankers, containing Accounts of their Bank Notes in Circulation, and of Gold Coin, to be inspected.

XXI. And whereas in order to ensure the rendering of true and faithful Accounts of the Amount of Bank Notes in Circulation, and the Amount of Gold and Silver Coin held by each Banker, as directed by this Act, it is necessary that the Commissioners of Stamps and Taxes should be empowered to cause the Books of Bankers issuing such Notes, and the Amount of Gold and Silver Coin held by such Bankers as aforesaid, to be inspected as herein-after mentioned; be it therefore enacted, That all and every the Book and Books of any Banker who shall issue Bank Notes under the Provisions of this Act, in which shall be kept, contained, or entered any Account, Minute, or Memorandum of or relating to the Bank Notes issued or to be issued by such Bank, of or relating to the Amount of such Notes in Circulation from Time to Time, or of or relating to the Gold or Silver Coin held by such Banker from Time to Time, or any Account, Minute, or Memorandum the Sight or Inspection whereof may tend to secure the rendering of true Accounts of the average Amount of such Notes in Circulation and Gold or Silver Coin held as directed by this Act, or to test the Truth of any such Account, shall be open for the Inspection and Examination at all seasonable Times of any Officer of Stamp Duties authorized in that Behalf by Writing signed by the Commissioners of Stamps and Taxes, or any Two of them; and every such Officer shall be at liberty to take Copies of or Extracts from any such Book or Account as aforesaid, and to inspect and ascertain the Amount of any Gold or Silver Coin held by such Banker; and if any Banker or other Person keeping any such Book, or having the Custody or Possession thereof or Power to produce the same, shall, upon Demand made by any such Officer showing (if required) his Authority in that Behalf, refuse to produce any such Book to such Officer for his Inspection and Examination, or to permit him to inspect and examine the same, or to take Copies thereof or Extracts therefrom, or of or from any such Account, Minute, or Memorandum as aforesaid, kept, contained, or entered therein, or if any Banker or other Person having the Custody or Possession of any Coin belonging to such Banker shall refuse to permit or prevent the Inspection of such Gold and Silver Coin as aforesaid, every such Banker or other Person so offending shall for every such Offence forfeit the Sum of One hundred Pounds: Provided always, that the said Commissioners shall not exercise the Powers aforesaid without the Consent of the Commissioners of Her Majesty's Treasury.

Penalty for refusing to allow such Inspection.

All Bankers to return their Names once a Year to the Stamp Office.

XXII. And be it enacted, That every Banker in *Ireland*, other than the Bank of *Ireland*, who is now carrying on or shall hereafter carry on Business as such, shall, on the First Day of *January* in each Year, or within Fifteen Days thereafter, make a Return to the Commissioners of Stamps and Taxes, at their Office in *Dublin*, of his Name, Residence, and Occupation, or, in the Case of a Company or Partnership, of the Name, Residence, and Occupation of every Person composing or being a Member of such Company or Partnership, and also the name of the Firm under which such Banker, Company, or Partnership carry on the Business of Banking, and of every Place where such Business is carried on; and if any such Banker shall omit or refuse to make such Return within Fifteen Days after the said First Day of *January*, or shall wilfully make other than a true Return of the Persons as herein required, every Banker so offending shall forfeit or pay the Sum of Fifty Pounds; and the said Commissioners of Stamps and Taxes shall on or before the First Day of *March* in every Year publish in the *Dublin Gazette* a Copy of the Return so made by every Banker.

XXIII. And be it enacted, That if the monthly average Circulation of Bank Notes of any Banker, taken in the Manner herein directed, shall at any Time exceed the Amount which such Banker is authorized to issue and to have in Circulation under the Provisions of this Act, such Banker shall in every such Case forfeit a Sum equal to the Amount by which the average monthly Circulation, taken as aforesaid, shall have exceeded the Amount which such Banker was authorized to issue and to have in Circulation as aforesaid.

XXIV. And be it enacted, That all Promissory or other Notes, Bills of Exchange or Drafts, or Undertakings in writing being negotiable or transferable, for the payment of any Sum or Sums of Money, or any Orders, Notes, or Undertakings in Writing, being negotiable or transferable, for the Delivery of any Goods, specifying their Value in Money less than the Sum of Twenty Shillings in the whole, heretofore made or issued, or which shall hereafter be made or issued in *Ireland*, shall, from and after the First Day of *January* One thousand eight hundred and forty-six, be and the same are hereby declared, to be absolutely void and of no Effect, any Law, Statute, Usage or Custom to the contrary thereof in anywise notwithstanding; and that if any Person or Persons shall, after the First Day of *January* One thousand eight hundred and forty-six, by any Art, Device, or Means whatsoever, publish or utter in *Ireland* any such Notes, Bills, Drafts, or Engagements as aforesaid, for a less Sum than Twenty Shillings, or on which less than the Sum of Twenty Shillings shall be due, and which shall be in anywise negotiable or transferable, or shall negotiate or transfer the same in *Ireland*, every such Person shall forfeit and pay for every such Offence any Sum not exceeding Twenty Pounds nor less than Five Pounds, at the Discretion of the Justice of the Peace who shall hear and determine such Offence.

XXV. And be it enacted, That all Promissory or other Notes, Bills of Exchange, or Drafts, or Undertakings in Writing, being negotiable or transferable, for the Payment of Twenty Shillings or any Sum of Money above that Sum and less than Five Pounds, or on which Twenty Shillings, or above that Sum and less than Five Pounds, shall remain undischarged, and which shall be issued within *Ireland* at any Time after the First Day of *January* One thousand eight hundred and forty-six shall specify the Names and

Places of Abode of the Persons respectively to whom or to whose Order the same shall be made payable, and shall bear Date before or at the Time of drawing or issuing thereof, and not on any Day subsequent thereto. and shall be made payable within the Space of Twenty-one Days next after the Date thereof, and shall not be transferable or negotiable after the Time hereby limited for Payment thereof, and that every Endorsement to be made thereon shall be made before the Expiration of that Time, and to bear Date at or not before the Time of making thereof, and shall specify the Name and Place of Abode of the Person or Persons to whom or to whose Order the Money contained in every such Note, Bill, Draft, or Undertaking is to be paid: and that the signing of every such Note, Bill, Draft, or Undertaking, and also of every such Endorsement, shall be attested by One subscribing Witness at the least; and which said Notes, Bills of Exchange, or Drafts, or Undertakings in Writing, may be made or drawn in Words to the Purport or Effect as set out in the Schedules to this Act annexed marked (D.) and (E.); and that all Promissory or other Notes, Bills of Exchange, or Drafts, or Undertakings in Writing, being negotiable or transferable, for the Payment of Twenty Shillings, or any Sum of Money above that Sum and less than Five Pounds, or in which Twenty Shillings, or above that Sum and less than Five Pounds, shall remain undischarged, and which shall be issued in *Ireland* at any Time after the said First Day of *January* One thousand eight hundred and forty-six, in any other manner than as aforesaid, and also every Endorsement on any such Note, Bill, Draft or other Undertaking to be negotiated under this Act, other than as aforesaid. shall and the same are hereby declared to be absolutely void, any Law, Statute, Usage, or Custom to the contrary thereof in anywise notwithstanding; provided that nothing in this Clause contained shall be construed to extend to any such Bank Notes as shall be lawfully issued by any Banker in *Ireland* authorized by this Act to continue the issue of Bank Notes.

Penalty for Persons other than Bankers hereby authorized issuing Notes payable on Demand for less than Five Pounds.

XXVI. And be it enacted, That if any Body Politic or Corporate or any Person or Persons shall, from and after the said First Day of *January* One thousand eight hundred and forty-six, make, sign, issue, or re-issue in *Ireland* any Promissory Note payable on Demand to the bearer thereof for any Sum of Money less than the Sum of Five Pounds, except the Bank Notes of such Bankers as are hereby authorized to continue to issue Bank Notes as aforesaid, then and in either of such Cases every such Body Politic or Corporate or Person or Persons so making, signing, issuing, or re-issuing any such Promissory Note as aforesaid, except as aforesaid, shall for every such Note so made, signed, issued, or re-issued forfeit the sum of Twenty Pounds.

Penalty for Persons other than Bankers

XXVII. And be it enacted, That if any Body Politic or Corporate or Person or Persons shall, from and after the passing of this Act, publish, utter, or negotiate in *Ireland* any Promissory or other Note (not being the

Bank Note of a Banker hereby authorized to continue to issue Bank Notes), or any Bill of Exchange, Draft, or Undertaking in Writing, being negotiable or transferable, for the payment of Twenty Shillings, or above that Sum and less than Five Pounds, or on which Twenty Shillings, or above that Sum and less than Five Pounds, shall remain undischarged, made, drawn, or endorsed in any other Manner than as is herein-before directed, and every such Body Politic or Corporate or Person or Persons so publishing, uttering, or negotiating any such Promissory or other Note (not being such Bank Note as aforesaid), Bill of Exchange, Draft, or Undertaking in Writing as aforesaid, shall forfeit and pay the Sum of Twenty Pounds.

XXVIII. Provided always, and be it enacted, That nothing herein contained shall extend to prohibit any Draft or Order drawn by any Person on his Banker, or on any Person acting as such Banker, for the Payment of Money held by such Banker or Person to the Use of the Person by whom such Draft or Order shall be drawn.

XXIX. And be it enacted, That all pecuniary Penalties under this Act may be sued or prosecuted for and recovered for the Use of Her Majesty, in the Name of Her Majesty's Attorney General or Solicitor General in *Ireland*, or of the Solicitor of Stamps in *Ireland*, or of any Person authorized to sue or prosecute for the same, by Writing under the Hands of the Commissioners of Stamps and Taxes, or in the Name of any Officer of Stamp Duties, by Action of Debt, Bill, Plaint, or Information in the Court of Exchequer in *Dublin*, or by Civil Bill in the Court of the Recorder, Chairman, or Assistant Barrister within whose local Jurisdiction any Offence shall have been committed, in respect of any such Penalty, or, in respect of any Penalty not exceeding Twenty Pounds, by Information or Complaint before One or more Justice or Justices of the Peace in *Ireland*, in such and the same Manner as any other Penalties imposed by any of the Laws now in force relating to the Duties under the Management of the Commissioners of Stamps; and it shall be lawful in all Cases for the Commissioners of Stamps and Taxes, either before or after any Proceedings commenced for Recovery of any such Penalty to mitigate or compound any such Penalty, as the said Commissioners shall think fit, and to stay any such Proceedings after the same shall have been commenced, and whether Judgment may have been obtained for such Penalty or not, on Payment of Part only of any such Penalty, with or without Costs, or on Payment only of the Costs incurred in such Proceedings, or of any Part thereof, or on such other Terms as such Commissioners shall judge reasonable: Provided always, that in no such Proceeding as aforesaid shall any Essoign, Protection, Wager of Law, nor more than One Imparlance be allowed; and all pecuniary Penalties imposed by or incurred under this Act, by whom or in whose Name soever the same shall be sued or prosecuted for or recovered, shall go and be applied to the Use of Her

Majesty, and shall be deemed to be and shall be accounted for as Part of Her Majesty's Revenue arising from Stamp Duties, any thing in any Act contained, or any Law or Usage, to the contrary in anywise notwithstanding: Provided always, that it shall be lawful for the Commissioners of Stamps and Taxes at their Discretion, to give all or any Part of such Penalties as Rewards to any Person or Persons who shall have detected the Offenders, or given Information which may have led to their Prosecution and Conviction.

Companies to sue and be sued in the Names of their Officers.

XXX. And be it enacted, That after the passing of this Act every Company or Copartnership of more than Six Persons established before the passing of this Act, for the Purpose of carrying on the Trade or Business of Bankers within the Distance of Fifty Miles from *Dublin*, shall have the same Powers and Privileges of suing and being sued, and of presenting Petitions to found Sequestations or Fiats in Bankruptcy, in the Name of any one of the public Officers of such Company or Copartnership, as the nominal Plaintiff, Petitioner, or Defendant, on behalf of such Company or Copartnership, as are provided with respect to Companies carrying on the said Trade or Business at any Place in *Ireland* exceeding the distance of Fifty Miles from *Dublin*, under the Provisions of an Act passed in the Sixth Year of the Reign of King *George* the Fourth, intituled *An Act for the better Regulation of Copartnerships of certain Bankers in* Ireland; and all Judgments, Decrees, and Orders made and obtained in any Action, Suit, or other Proceeding brought, instituted, or carried on by or against any such Company or Copartnership carrying on Business within the Distance of Fifty Miles from *Dublin*, in the Name of their public Officer, shall have the same Effect and Operation, and may be enforced in like Manner in all respects as is provided in and by the last-mentioned Act, with respect to the Judgments, Decrees and Orders therein mentioned; provided that every such Company or Copartnership as last aforesaid shall make out and deliver from Time to Time to the Commissioners of Stamps and Taxes the several Accounts or Returns required by the last-mentioned Act; and all the Provisions of the last-mentioned Act as to such Accounts or Returns shall be taken to apply to the Accounts or Returns so made out and delivered by the said last-mentioned Companies, as if they had been originally included in the Provisions of the last-mentioned Act.

6 G. 4. c. 42.

Provision in case of Determination of existing Agreement between Bank of Ireland and Tipperary Joint Stock Bank.

XXXI. And whereas a certain Joint Stock Banking Company, called and known as "The *Tipperary* Joint Stock Bank," refrained from issuing its own Bank Notes under a certain Agreement with the Governor and Company of the Bank of *Ireland* for the Issue of the Bank Notes of the said Governor and Company, which Agreement is determinable by either Party upon certain Notice to the other Party, and it is just that in case such Agreement should at any Time hereafter during the Continuance of this Act be determined and put an end to by the Governor and Company of the Bank of *Ireland*, that the said *Tipperary* Joint Stock Bank should receive by way of Compensation such Composition as hereafter mentioned; be it therefore enacted, That if the said Agreement shall be at any Time hereafter during the Continuance of this Act determined or put an end to by the Governor and Company of the Bank of *Ireland* then and in such Case the said Governor and Company shall from the Termination of the said Agreement pay and allow to the said *Tipperary* Joint Stock Bank, so long as the latter shall continue to carry on the Business of a Bank and to issue exclusively the Notes of the Governor and Company of the Bank of *Ireland*, a Composition at and after the Rate of One *per Centum per Annum* on the average annual Amount of the Bank of *Ireland* Notes issued by the said *Tipperary* Joint Stock Bank, and kept in Circulation, such average annual Amount to be ascertained by the Bank of *Ireland* in the Manner provided for regulating the Compensation to be made to certain Bankers by the Bank of *England* in and by the Act passed in the Seventh and Eighth Years of the Reign of Her present Majesty, intituled *An Act to regulate the Issue of Bank Notes, and for giving to the Governor and Company of the Bank of* England *certain Privileges for a limited Period:* Provided always, that the total Sum payable to the *Tipperary* Joint Stock Bank by way of Composition as aforesaid in any One Year shall not exceed One *per Cent.* on an Amount that hath been agreed on by and between the Bank of *Ireland* and the *Tipperary* Joint Stock Bank and certified by both Banks to the Commissioners of Stamps and Taxes; and such Composition shall cease to be payable from and after the First Day of *January* One thousand eight hundred and fifty-six.

XXXII. And be it enacted, That the Term "Bank Note" used in this Act shall extend and apply to all Bills or Notes for the Payment of Money to the Bearer on Demand; and that the Term "Banker" shall, when the Bank of *Ireland* be not specially excepted, extend and apply to the Governor and Company of the Bank of *Ireland*, and to all other Corporations, Societies, Partnerships, and Persons, and every individual Person carrying on the Business of Banking, whether by the Issue of Bank Notes or otherwise; and that the Word "Coin" shall be construed to mean the Coin of this Realm; and that the Word "Person" used in this Act shall include Corporations; and that the Singular Number used in this Act shall include the Plural Number, and the Plural Number the Singular, except where there is anything in the Context repugnant to such Construction; and that the Masculine Gender in this Act shall include the Feminine, except where there is anything in the Context repugnant to such Construction.

XXXIII. And be it enacted, That this Act may be amended or repealed by any Act to be passed in the present Session of Parliament.

SCHEDULES referred to in the foregoing Act.

SCHEDULE (A.)

Name and Title set forth in Licence - - ______________________Bank.

Name of the Firm - - - - - - ______________________Firm.

Head Offices or principal Places of Issue - ______________________Place.

AMOUNT of NOTES in Circulation on Saturday the Day of { £5 and upwards - £
Under £5 - - £ ________

TOTAL - - £ ________

AMOUNT of GOLD and SILVER COIN held at the head Office or principal Place of Issue at the Close of Business on—

	Head Office at		Head Office at		Head Office at		Head Office at	
	Gold.	Silver.	Gold.	Silver.	Gold.	Silver.	Gold.	Silver.
Monday the								
Tuesday the								
Wednesday the								
Thursday the								
Friday the								
Saturday the								

TOTAL AMOUNT of COIN held at the Close of Business on Saturday the

Day of 18 .

Gold	- - - -	£
Silver	- - - -	£
TOTAL	- -	£

[*To be inserted in the Account at the End of each Period of Four Weeks.*]

Amount of Notes authorized by Certificate	- - -	£
Average Amount of Notes in Circulation during the Four Weeks ending as above	£5 and upwards	£
	Under £5 - -	£
Average Amount of Coin held during the said Four Weeks - - - - -	Gold - -	£
	Silver -	£
	TOTAL - -	£

I, being the [Banker, Chief Cashier, Director, *or* Partner, *as the Case may be*], do hereby certify, That the above is a true Account of the Notes in Circulation, and of the Coin held by the said Bank, as required under the Act 8 & 9 Vict.

(Signed)____________________

Dated this Day of 18

SCHEDULE (B.)

Name and Title, as set forth in the Licence.	Name of the Firm.	Head Office or principal Place of Issue.	Circulation authorized by Certificate.	Average Circulation during Four Weeks ending the			Average Amount of Coin held during Four Weeks ending		
				£5 and upwards.	Under £5.	TOTAL.	Gold.	Silver.	TOTAL.

I hereby certify, That each of the Bankers named in the above Return who have in Circulation an Amount of Notes beyond that authorized in their Certificate [with the Exception of *A.B. or C.D., as the Case may be,*] have held an Amount of Gold and Silver Coin not less than that which they are required to hold during the Period to which this Return relates.

Dated this Day of 18 .

(Signed) ________________ Officer of Stamp Duties.

SCHEDULE (D.)

[*Place*] [*Day*] [*Month*] [*Year*]

Twenty-one Days after Date I promise to pay to *A.B.* of [*Place*], or his Order, the Sum of for Value received by

Witness, *E.F.* *C.D.*

And the Endorsement, toties quoties.

[*Day*] [*Month*] [*Year*]

Pay the Contents to *G.H.* of [*Place*], or his Order.

Witness, *J.K.* *A.B.*

SCHEDULE (E.)

[*Place*] [*Day*] [*Month*] [*Year*]

Twenty-one Days after Date pay to *A.B.* of [*Place*], or his Order, the Sum of Value received, as advised by

To *E.F.* of [*Place*]. *C.D.*

Witness, *G.H.*

And the Endorsement, toties quoties.

[*Day*] [*Month*] [*Year*]

Pay the Contents to *J.K.* of [*Place*], or his Order.

Witness, *L.M.* *A.B.*

A COPY OF THE CHARTER

Of the Corporation of the

GOVERNOR AND COMPANY OF THE BANK OF IRELAND.

Recital of the Act for establishing the Bank of Ireland.

GEORGE THE THIRD, by the Grace of God, of *Great Britain, France*, and *Ireland*, King, Defender of the Faith, and so forth, To all unto whom these presents shall come, GREETING, WHEREAS in and by a certain Act, lately made in our Parliament of *Ireland*, entitled, *An Act for establishing a Bank*, by the Name of "THE GOVERNOR AND COMPANY OF THE BANK OF IRELAND," It is amongst other things enacted, that it should and might be lawful to and for us, by Commission under the Great Seal of *Ireland*, to authorize and appoint any number of persons, to take and receive all such voluntary Subscriptions as should be made on or before the first day of *January*, in the year 1784, by any Person or Persons, Natives or Foreigners, Bodies Politic or Corporate, for and towards the raising and paying into the receipt of our Treasury of *Ireland*, the sum of Six Hundred Thousand Pounds sterling, to be paid in Money, or by Debentures which have been or shall be issued from our said Treasury by virtue of any Act or Acts of Parliament theretofore, or in the then present Sessions of Parliament, made in our kingdom of *Ireland*, bearing an Interest at the rate of Four Pounds *per centum per annum*, which Debentures should be taken at par, and considered as Money, by the persons to whom the same should be paid; for which sum so to be subscribed, a sum by way of Annuity, equal in amount to the Interest upon the said Debentures, at the rate of Four Pounds *per centum per annum*, should be paid at our Treasury in manner in the said Act mentioned: And that it should and might be lawful for us, by our Letters Patent, under the Great Seal of *Ireland*, to limit, direct, and appoint, how, and in what manner and proportions, and under what Rules and Directions the said sum of Six Hundred Thousand Pounds sterling, and every, or any part or proportion thereof may be assignable or transferable, assigned or transferred, to such person or persons only, as shall freely and voluntarily accept the same, and not otherwise; and to incorporate all, and every such Subscribers and Contributors, their Executors, Administrators, Successors or Assignees, to be one Body Corporate and Politic, by the Name of "THE GOVERNOR AND COMPANY OF THE BANK OF IRELAND," to have perpetual succession, and with such privileges and powers, and to be under such Rules as are therein mentioned; subject nevertheless, to a certain proviso or condition of redemption in the said Act contained. AND it is thereby further enacted, that no one Person, or Body Politic or Corporate, should by himself, herself, or themselves, or by any person in trust for him, her, or them, subscribe towards raising the said sum of Six Hundred Thousand Pounds sterling, any sum or sums of Money, exceeding the sum of Ten Thousand Pounds sterling, for the use of such Person, or Body Politic or Corporate respectively: And that every such Subscriber should at the time of such Subscription, pay, or cause to be paid, under the Commissioners who should be authorized to receive Subscriptions as aforesaid, one full fourth part of his, her, or their respective Subscriptions; and that in default of such payment, every such Subscription shall be void; and that the residue of such Subscription shall be paid into our said Treasury, in such manner and proportions, and at such times, before the first day of *January*, which shall be in the year 1784, as such Commissioners shall direct and appoint: And in default of any such Payments, that then such parts as shall have been paid, shall be forfeited to and for the benefit of the said Bank, to be applied as in the said Act is mentioned. AND it is thereby further enacted, that in case the whole sum of Six Hundred Thousand Pounds sterling should not be subscribed, on or before the first day of *January*, which shall be in the year of our Lord 1784, that the said Powers for erecting the said Corporation should cease; and that in such case the said subscribers should be intitled to, and receive from the said Commissioners, such or like Debentures, or such sums of Money as shall have been by them subscribed and paid, with all Interest accruing upon the said Debentures, during the time the same shall have been deposited with the said Commissioners; and that the said sum of Six Hundred Thousand Pounds sterling, when paid by the said Subscribers, shall be the *common capital Stock of the said Bank.* And that all and every Debenture and Debentures subscribed in part, or for the whole of the said Stock, shall, as soon as the same shall be deposited by the said Subscribers, be locked up in a Chest in our said Treasury until the same shall be cancelled: And that from and after the passing our said Letters Patent, all and every such Debentures shall be cancelled by our Vice-Treasurer of *Ireland*, his Deputy or Deputies, in the presence of the Governor and Company of the said Bank, from which day all Interest payable on the said Debentures shall cease, and in lieu thereof, there shall be paid and payable out of the Funds made applicable by Parliament for payment of Interest on said Debentures, one annuity or yearly sum of *Twenty-four Thousand Pounds sterling*, to be paid by half yearly payments to the said Governor and Company of the said Bank, as is in the said Act mentioned; and that the said annual sum of *Twenty-four Thousand Pounds sterling*, shall be applied to the uses of all the members of the said Corporation for the time being, rateably to each Member's share of, and interest in, the Common Capital Stock of the said Governor and Company, pursuant to such Rules as should be specified by our said Letters Patent. AND WHEREAS, in pursuance of the said Act, we did by our Commission, or Letters Patent, under the Great Seal of *Ireland*, bearing date at *Dublin*, the twenty-seventh day of *July* now last past, nominate, constitute, authorize, and appoint our trusty and well beloved, the Right Honourable *Joseph Earl of Milltown*, [*Here follow the names of the rest of the Commissioners*] or any three or more of them, to be our COMMISSIONERS, to take and receive all such voluntary Subscriptions as should be made on or before the said first day of *January*, in the year of our Lord 1784, by any Person or Persons, Natives or Foreigners, or by or for any Body Politic or Corporate, for, and towards the raising and paying of the said sum of Six Hundred Thousand Pounds sterling, in manner in the said *Act* mentioned, with Power and Direction to them, or such, or so many of them as are thereby authorized and appointed to take such Subscriptions; and also to direct and appoint in what manner the residue of such Subscriptions should be paid in, and to do and perform such matters and things in relation thereunto as are thereby enjoined. AND we did in and by the same Commission, *promise and declare*, that in case the said sum of Six Hundred Thousand Pounds sterling should be subscribed and paid *before the first said day of January, in the said year* 1784, that then We, our Heirs or Successors, should, and would immediately after the said first day of *January*, 1784, or so soon as Six Hundred Thousand Pounds sterling should be subscribed and paid as aforesaid, (which of them should first happen) *grant, and make forth our Royal Charter, or Letters Patent*, under the Great Seal of IRELAND, and thereby incorporate all and every such Subscribers and Contributors who should be then living, and who should not have assigned their Interest in their said Subscriptions; and in case any of them should be dead, the Executors or Administrators of such Subscribers: AND in case any of the said Subscribers should have assigned their Interest in their said Subscriptions, in all such cases the Assignees of such Subscribers to be *one Body Corporate and Politic*, by the Name of the GOVERNOR AND COMPANY OF THE BANK OF IRELAND, with such Powers, Capacities, Privileges, Benefits, Liberties and Advantages, and under and subject to such Rules, Restrictions, Power of Redemption, Provisoes, Limitations and Clauses as are therein mentioned or referred unto. AND we did thereby for us, our Heirs and Successors, declare, limit, and appoint, that all and every person and persons, his, her, and their Executors, Administrators, Successors and Assignees, according and in proportion to the sum or sums of Money by him, her, or them, respectively subscribed and paid, should have and be deemed to have an Interest or Share in the said Stock of Six Hundred Thousand Pounds sterling, and the Annuity granted by the said *Act;* and that such Interest or Share, or any Part thereof, should be assignable and transferable, and should and might be assigned and transferred, by any person or persons intitled thereunto, to any other person or persons, and so over, as fully and effectually as any other Interest whatsoever, is by Law assignable; so as such Assignments or Transfers which should be made on or before the full and complete subscribing and paying the said Sum of Six Hundred Thousand Pounds sterling, and before the granting of such our Charter of Incorporation, should be entered or registered in the Office of our *Auditor-General in Ireland, within Thirty-one Days after making the said respective Assignments or*

Transfers, and all such Assignments or Transfers, which should be made after the granting of our said Charter of Incorporation, should be made, entered and registered, in such manner and form, and at such places, as in and by the said *Act* and by our *Royal Letter is directed*, and as in and by the said *Charter of Incorporation*, shall be directed and appointed. AND, we did thereby order and direct our said *Commissioners*, when and so often as they should receive any Sums for or towards said Subscription, to pay the same forthwith into our *Treasury*. AND, in the said Commission, are contained several other powers, directions, agreements, clauses, matters and things, as in and by the same, relation being thereunto had, more fully and at large appears. AND WHEREAS, several sums, amounting in the whole to the sum of Six Hundred Thousand Pounds sterling, have been subscribed, and the first fourth part thereof paid by such Debentures as aforesaid, to our said *Commissioners or some of them*, pursuant to the said *Act of Parliament*, on or before the 25th day of *December* last past, by or for *David Latouche* Esq.; [*Here the names of the several other Subscribers are inserted.*] AND three or more of our said Commissioners being a competent and sufficient number, did direct and require that the residue of the said Subscriptions should be paid into our said Treasury, on or before the first day of *March*, in the year of our Lord 1783; and the same was accordingly, on or before the said last mentioned day, paid by Debentures into our said Treasury. AND WHEREAS, we being desirous to promote the *public good and benefit of our people, and to advance the credit of our said Kingdom of* Ireland, *and the extension of its Trade and Commerce*, which in these presents are chiefly designed and intended, as well as the profit and advantage of all such as have subscribed and contributed, according to the said Act of Parliament and our said Commission thereupon issued, their Executors, Administrators, Successors, and Assignees, respectively; and, in pursuance as well of the powers and clauses for this purpose contained in the said Act of Parliament, as of our gracious promise and declaration, made in and by our said Commission or Letters Patent, under the great seal of *Ireland*, whereby the Subscriptions and Contributions on the said Act have been promoted or encouraged; and, by virtue of our Prerogative Royal; KNOW YE, THEREFORE, that we, of our special grace certain knowledge, and mere motion, by and with the advice and consent of our right trusty, and right well beloved cousin and counsellor, GEORGE GRENVILLE NUGENT TEMPLE, EARL TEMPLE, our Lieutenant General and General Governor of our said Kingdom of *Ireland*, have, in pursuance of the said *Act*, and according to the tenor and effect of *our Letters*, under our *Privy Signet* and *Royal Sign Manual*, bearing date at our court, at *St. James's*, the 16th day of *April*, 1783, in the twenty-third year of our Reign, and now inrolled in the Rolls of our High Court of Chancery in our said Kingdom of *Ireland*, HAVE given, granted, made, ordained, constituted, declared, appointed, and established for us, our Heirs and Successors, that the said *David Latouche*, [*Here the Names of the rest of the Subscribers are repeated.*] and all and every other Person and Persons, *Natives* and *Foreigners*, *Bodies Politic* or

Corporate, who over and above the Persons before especially named, HAVE at any time or times before the making of our said *Letters Patent*, subscribed and contributed any sum or sums of Money towards the said sum of Six Hundred Thousand Pounds sterling so subscribed and paid, pursuant to the said Act and our said Commission, and who are now living or existent, and have not assigned their Interests in the said Subscriptions, and all and every the Executors, Administrators and Successors of any of the said Original Subscribers who are now dead, and have not in their life times assigned their Interest in the said Subscriptions, and the Executors and Administrators and Successors of such of the said Assignees who are now dead, and did not in their life times assign or part with their Interests in the said Stock and Annual Fund; and all and every Person and Persons, *Natives* or *Foreigners*, *Bodies Politic* and *Corporate*, who either as *Original Subscribers* of the said sum of Six Hundred Thousand Pounds sterling so subscribed, and not having parted with their Interests in their Subscriptions, or as Executors or Administrators, Successors or Assignees, or by any other lawful Title derived or to be derived from, by, or under the said Original Subscribers of the said sum of Six Hundred Thousand Pounds sterling, or any of them, now have, or at any time or times hereafter shall have or be entitled to any Part, Share or Interest, of or in the *principal or capital Stock* of the said *Corporation*, or the said yearly Fund of Twenty-Four Thousand Pounds sterling granted by the said *Act* of Parliament, or any part thereof, so long as they respectively shall have any such Part, Share, or Interest therein, and no longer, shall be and be called *one Body Politic and Corporate of themselves*, in Deed and in Name, by the Name of "THE GOVERNOR AND COMPANY OF THE BANK OF IRELAND;" and them, by that Name *one Body Politic and Corporate*, in Deed and in Name, OUR WILL AND PLEASURE IS, AND WE DO FOR US, OUR HEIRS AND SUCCESSORS, make, create, erect, establish and confirm for ever by these Presents, and by the same Name, they and their Successors shall have perpetual *succession*, and shall have and may have and use a *common Seal* for the use, business, or affairs of the said *Body Politic and Corporate*, and their Successors, with power to break, alter, and to make anew their Seal from time to time at their pleasure, and as they shall see cause; and by the same Name they and their Successors in all times coming, shall be able and capable in Law to have, take, *purchase*, receive, hold, keep, possess, enjoy and retain to them and their Successors, any Manors, Messuages, Lands, Rents, Tenements, Liberties, Privileges, Franchises, Hereditaments and Possessions whatsoever, and of what kind, nature, or quality soever: AND moreover to purchase and acquire all Goods and Chattels whatsoever, wherein they are not restrained by the said *Act*; and also to sell, grant, demise, alien and dispose of the same Manors, Messuages, Lands, Rents, Tenements, Privileges, Franchises, Hereditaments, Possessions, Goods and Chattels, or any of them, and by the same Name they and their Successors shall and may *sue and implead, and be sued and impleaded*, answer and defend, and be answered and defended in Courts of Record, or any other place whatsoever, and before whatsoever Judges,

May have a common Seal.

May purchase and hold.

May sue and be sued.

Justices, Officers and Ministers, of us, our Heirs and Successors, in all and singular *Pleas, Actions, Suits, Causes and Demands* whatsoever, of what kind, nature, or sort soever, and in as large, ample and beneficial manner and form as any other Body Politic and Corporate, or any other the Liege People of Ireland, or other our Dominions, being persons able and capable in Law, may or can have, take, purchase, receive, hold, keep, possess, enjoy, sell, grant, demise, alien, dispose, sue, implead, defend or answer, or be sued, impleaded, defended or answered in any manner of wise; and shall and may do and execute all and singular other matters and things by the Name aforesaid, that to them shall or may appertain to do by virtue of the said *Act* or otherwise; *subject* nevertheless *to the proviso and condition of redemption in the said Act mentioned*, and to all and every other Clauses, Provisoes and Conditions in the said Act contained. AND OUR FURTHER WILL AND PLEASURE IS, and we do hereby declare, that all persons having any Interest or Part in the Capital Stock or Fund of the said Corporation, either as *Original Subscribers* or by *Assignments*, or as *Executors or Administrators or otherwise*, shall be and be esteemed *Members* of the said Corporation, and shall be admitted into the same without any fee or charge whatsoever. AND OUR FURTHER WILL AND PLEASURE IS, and we do hereby for us, our Heirs and Successors, declare, limit, direct and appoint that the aforesaid sum of Six Hundred Thousand Pounds sterling so subscribed as aforesaid, shall be and be called, accepted, esteemed, reputed and taken, to be the *common Capital and principal Stock* of the Corporation hereby constituted; and all and every Person and Persons, his, her, and their Executors and Administrators, Successors and Assignees, according and in proportion to the sum or sums of Money by him, her, or them respectively subscribed as aforesaid, shall have and be deemed to have an Interest or Share in the said *Principal Stock*, and of and in the yearly Fund of Twenty-four Thousand Pounds sterling granted by the said *Act* of Parliament. AND OUR FURTHER WILL AND PLEASURE IS, and we do hereby for us, our Heirs and Successors, authorize, enjoin and require our *Vice-Treasurer* or *Vice-Treasurers*, *Pay-Master* or *Pay-Masters General* of our said kingdom of *Ireland* for the time being, his or their Deputy or Deputies, without any further or other Warrant to be had or obtained from us, our Heirs or Successors, to direct their Warrants and Orders according to the said *Act*, for the payment of the said yearly sum of Twenty-four Thousand Pounds sterling, by, and out of the said Monies appointed for the payment of the said yearly Fund of Twenty-four Thousand Pounds sterling to the said *Governor and Company of the Bank of Ireland* and their Successors; under, and subject nevertheless, to the payment of the issues, fines, amerciaments and debts upon *Judgments* against the said *Corporation*, according to the purport of the said *Act*. AND for the better *ordering*, *managing* and *governing* the said Stock and other Affairs of the said Corporation, and for the making and establishing a continual succession of persons to be Governor, Deputy-Governor, and Directors of the said Corporation, OUR WILL AND PLEASURE IS, and we do by these presents for us, our Heirs and Successors, grant unto the said *Governor and Company of the Bank of Ireland*, and their Successors, and do hereby ordain and appoint, that there shall be from time to time, for ever (of the said Members of the said Company) a GOVERNOR, a DEPUTY-GOVERNOR, and *fifteen* DIRECTORS, of, and in the said *Corporation;* which Governor, Deputy-Governor, and Directors, or any *eight, or more of them*, (of whom the *Governor* or *Deputy-Governor*, unless as herein after is excepted, to be always one) shall be and be called a *Court of Directors*, for the ordering, managing and directing the Affairs of the said Corporation, and shall have such powers and privileges as are herein after mentioned: AND we do hereby nominate, constitute, ordain and appoint, that *David Latouche*, Esq., the younger, shall be the present and first Governor; and that *Theophilus Thompson*, Esq., shall be the present and first Deputy-Governor; and that *Alexander Jaffray*, Esq.; *Travers Hartley*, Esq.; Sir *Nicholas Lawless*, Baronet; *Amos Strettle*, Esq.; *Jeremiah Vickers*, Esq.; *John Latouche*, Esq.; *Abraham Wilkinson*, Esq.; *George Godfrey Hoffman*, Esq.; *William Colvill*, Esq.; *Peter Latouche*, Esq.; *Samuel Dick*, Esq.; *Jeremiah D'Olier*, Esq.; *Alexander Armstrong*, Esq.; *George Palmer*, Esq.; and *John Allen*, Esq.; shall be the present and first Directors of the said Corporation; and the said Governor, Deputy-Governor, and Directors, shall continue in their present respective Offices until the twenty-fifth day of *March*, which shall be in the year of our Lord 1784, and until others shall be duly chosen in their respective Offices, and *sworn* into the same; unless they, or any of them, shall sooner die or be removed, as herein after mentioned. PROVIDED ALWAYS, and our Will and Pleasure is, and we do direct, that, at no Annual Election, there shall be chosen for Directors for the ensuing year above *two-thirds* of those who were Directors for the year next preceding. AND OUR WILL AND PLEASURE IS, AND WE DO FURTHER, by these presents, for us, our Heirs and Successors, give and grant unto the said Governor and Company of the *Bank of Ireland*, AND we do hereby ordain, will, and appoint, that it shall and may be lawful to and for all and every the Members of the said Corporation, or Body Politic, from time to time, to assemble and meet together at any convenient place or places, for the choice of their Governor, Deputy-Governor, and Directors; and for the making of Bye-Laws, Ordinances, Rules, Orders or Directions, for the Government of the said Corporation, and for any other Affairs or Business concerning the same; *public notice thereof being first given* by writing, to be affixed upon the Royal Exchange in *Dublin*, *two days at least* before the time appointed for such meeting; and that all the Members of the said Corporation, or so many of them as shall be so assembled, shall be, and be called *A General Court of the said Corporation*, which shall meet and assemble at such times, and in such manner, as herein after is directed; and that all

First Governor.

First Deputy-Governor. First fifteen Directors.

Continuance in their Offices.

Not above two-thirds of the Directors the preceding year to be re-elected.*

Power to assemble.

Notice of General Courts.

* Repealed by Act 35 and 36 Vict., cap 5 (1872), which also gives power to reduce the number of Directors.

succeeding Governors, Deputy-Governors and Directors of the said Corporation, shall, from and after the five and twentieth day of *March*, in the year of our Lord 1784, be yearly and successively chosen for ever out of the Members of the said Corporation, on some day or days, or times, between the five and twentieth day of *March*, and twenty-fifth day of *April* in every year, by the Majority of Votes, of all and every of the Members of the Corporation, having then, each of them, in their own right, Five Hundred Pounds sterling, or more, Share or Interest in the said Capital Stock and Fund of the said Corporation; and who shall be personally present at such Elections, every of them having a Share amounting to Five Hundred Pounds sterling or more, to have, and give *one vote*, and no more; which succeeding Governors, Deputy-Governors and Directors so chosen, shall severally and respectively continue in their respective Offices, to which they shall be severally elected *for one year, and until others shall be duly chosen and sworn into their places respectively.* PROVIDED NEVERTHELESS, that in case of death, avoidance, or removal of the Governor, Deputy-Governor, or any of the Directors of the said Corporation for the time being, the Survivors of them, or the Majority of those remaining in their Offices, shall and may at any time assemble together the Members of the said Corporation, in order to elect other persons, by Members qualified to vote in manner aforesaid, in the room of those *dead, removed, or avoided*; and that every Deputy-Governor (in the absence of the Governor) shall have the same power as a Governor: PROVIDED NEVERTHELESS, and our Will and Pleasure is, and we do hereby ordain, constitute and appoint, and command, that no person or persons, shall be, or be esteemed qualified or capable to be an Elector to vote, or shall give any vote at any General Court or otherwise, for an election of Governor, Deputy-Governor or Directors, or any of them; or for, or concerning the making of *Bye-Laws* or in any other matter relating to the Affairs or Government of the said Corporation, who shall not have at the time of such General Court, and have had for *six calendar Months previous thereto*, in his, her, or their name and right, and for his or their own use, and not in trust for any other, *Five Hundred Pounds* sterling or more, Share or interest in the said *capital Stock* of the said Corporation, unless such Capital Stock shall become the property of such person or persons *by marriage, by bequest, or by virtue of the Statute for distributing the personal property of Intestates;* and who also shall not at the time of holding any such *General Court*, take the Oath herein after mentioned, if required thereunto by any Member or Members of the said Corporation then present, having each Five Hundred Pounds sterling, Share or Interest at least, in the said *capital Stock*, before the Governor, Deputy-Governor, or any two or more of the Directors of the said Corporation, viz.: "*I, A. B. do swear that the sum of* Five Hundred Pounds sterling *of the* Capital Stock *of the Body Politic, called by the Name of* The Governor and Company of the Bank of Ireland, *doth at this time belong to me, and hath for the space of six calendar Months belonged to me in my own right, and not in trust, for any other person or persons;*" but in case such Stock shall have come by marriage, bequest, or under the said

Statute for distributing the personal property of Intestates, then the words following, to wit, "*and hath belonged to me for the space of six calendar Months*" shall be omitted; and instead thereof, shall be inserted the words following, to wit, "*and hath come to me by marriage, bequest, or under the statute for distributing the personal property of Intestates.*" AND we do hereby constitute, ordain, and appoint, that no one Member of the said Corporation, shall in any election of Governor, Deputy-Governor, Director or other Officer of the said Corporation, or in any the Business or Affairs of the said Corporation, have, or give any more than *one vote*, whatever his Share or Interest in the said Capital Stock shall be. PROVIDED NEVERTHELESS, that any person or persons, commonly called or known to be *Quakers*, who at the time of holding any such General Court as aforesaid, shall have Five Hundred Pounds sterling, Interest or Share, or more in the said Capital Stock; and shall then, if thereunto required by any Member or Members of the said Corporation then present, having each Five Hundred Pounds sterling, Share, or Interest at least, in the said Capital Stock, make and sign *a solemn declaration to the effect as aforesaid, as the case shall require*, shall be capable of having a Vote at any General Court of the said Corporation. AND OUR WILL AND PLEASURE IS, and we do by these presents, for us, our Heirs, and Successors, give full power and authority to the Governor, Deputy-Governor, or any two or more of the Directors of the said Corporation, for the time being, to give and administer the said *Oath and Declaration respectively* to the said Members; and do hereby order and direct them to administer the same accordingly. PROVIDED FURTHER, and our Will and Pleasure is, and we do hereby for us, our Heirs, and Successors, ordain and appoint, that no person shall at any time be capable of being chosen a *Governor* of the said Corporation, unless he shall at the time of such Election, be our *natural-born subject, or naturalized*; and shall also then have in his own name, in his own right, and for his own use, Four Thousand Pounds sterling or more, in the Capital Stock of the said Corporation; and that no person shall at any time be capable of being *chosen Deputy-Governor* of the said Corporation, unless he shall at the time of such Election, be our *natural-born subject, or naturalized*; and shall then also have in his own name, in his own right, and for his own use, Three Thousand Pounds sterling, or more, in the *capital Stock* of the said Corporation; and that no person shall be capable of being chosen a *Director* of the said Corporation, who shall not, at the time of such choice, be our *natural-born subject, or naturalized*; and shall also then have in his own name, in his own right, and for his own use, Two Thousand Pounds sterling, or more, in the said Capital Stock; and that no Governor, Deputy-Governor, or Directors, shall continue in his, or their respective Offices, longer than the continuance of such their respective Interests and Stock in their own names and rights, and to their uses respectively; but upon parting with, or reducing his, or their respective Share or Interest in the *capital Stock*, to any lesser sum or sums than as aforesaid, the said respective Offices or Places of such *Governor, Deputy-Governor*, or *Director*, so parting with, reducing, or diminishing their said

None to have above one Vote.

Proviso for Quakers.

Power to administer the Oaths and Declaration to Electors.

Qualification of Governor.

Qualification of Deputy-Governor.

Qualification of Directors.

Office vacant by lessening Stock.

Shares or Interests as aforesaid, shall cease, determine, and become vacant, and others to be chosen in their room, by a *General Court* of the said *Corporation.* PROVIDED ALSO, and our Will and Pleasure is, and we do by these presents, for us, our Heirs and Successors, will ordain and appoint, that the said *David Latouche*, the younger, hereby nominated to be the first Governor, and every person hereafter to be chosen to the said Office, or Trust of Governor of the said Corporation, shall not be capable of executing or acting in the said Office, or Trust of Governor at any time, until he shall have made and subscribed the *Declaration*, pursuant to an *Act* of Parliament made in the Kingdom of *Ireland*, entitled, "An *Act* to prevent the further growth of *Popery;*" and shall also have taken the *Oaths of Allegiance, Supremacy, and Abjuration*, and shall not be capable of executing of, or acting in the said Office, or Trust of Governor, at any time or times hereafter, until he shall have taken the Oath following, to wit. "*I, A. B. do swear that the sum of* Four Thousand Pounds sterling, *of the capital Stock of the Body Politic called by the Name of* The Governor and Company of the Bank of Ireland, *whereof I am appointed or elected to be Governor, doth at this time belong to me in my own right, and not in trust for any other person or persons;*" and likewise another Oath in the form, or to the effect following, that is to say, "*I, A. B. being nominated, or elected, to be Governor of the* Company of the Bank of Ireland, *do promise and swear that I will, to the utmost of my power by all lawful ways and means, endeavour to support and maintain the Body Politic of the* Governor and Company of the Bank of Ireland, *and the Liberties and Privileges thereof; and that in the execution of the said Office of Governor, I will faithfully and honestly demean myself according to the best of my skill and understanding.*—So help me God." Which Oaths and Declaration of the first and present Governor above named, shall, and may be administered, and received by the *Chancellor of our said Kingdom of* Ireland, *or the Keeper or Commissioners of our* Great Seal *of* Ireland, *or by the Chancellor or Chief Baron of our Court of Exchequer in* Ireland, or any of them for the time being; and to and from any *future Governor*, shall, and may be administered, and received by the Chancellor of our said Kingdom of *Ireland*, or by the Keeper or Commissioners of the Great Seal of *Ireland*, or by the Chancellor or Chief Baron of the Court of Exchequer in *Ireland;* for the time being, *or by the Governor or Deputy-Governor of the said Corporation for the last preceding year;* or (in case a Deputy-Governor shall be then sworn into his Office) then by such Deputy-Governor. AND OUR WILL AND PLEASURE IS, and we do hereby for us, our Heirs and Successors, direct, authorize and appoint, the Chancellor of *Ireland*, and the Keeper or Commissioners of the Great Seal of *Ireland*, Chancellor or Chief Baron of the Court of Exchequer in *Ireland*, or any of them, for the time being, or such preceding Governor, or preceding Deputy-Governor, or such Deputy-Governor so qualified, as aforesaid, to administer and receive the said *Oaths and Declaration*, to and from every or any such person appointed or elected to be Governor of the said Corporation, as aforesaid. PROVIDED ALSO, and our Will and Pleasure is, and we do hereby for us, our Heirs and Successors.

the like Oaths to be taken by the Deputy-Governor.

ordain and appoint that the said *Theophilus Thompson*, hereby nominated, constituted and appointed, to be the first *Deputy-Governor*; or any person hereafter to be chosen to the Office or Trust of Deputy-Governor of the said Corporation, shall not be capable of executing or acting in the said Office or Trust of Deputy-Governor, until he shall have taken *the like Oaths and made the like Declaration (mutatis mutandis)*, as are before prescribed, to be taken and made by the Governor; which Oath and Declaration, to and from the first Deputy-Governor, above

How administered.

named, shall, and may be administered, and received, by the Chancellor of our said Kingdom of *Ireland*, or Keeper or Commissioners of our Great Seal of *Ireland*, or by the Chancellor or Chief Baron of our Court of Exchequer in *Ireland*, *or by the first Governor of the said Corporation*, after he shall himself be first sworn in as aforesaid; and to and from *any future* Deputy-Governor, shall and may be administered, and received by the Chancellor of our said Kingdom of *Ireland*, or by the Keeper or Commissioners of the Great Seal of *Ireland*, or by the Chancellor or Chief Baron of our Court of Exchequer in *Ireland*, for the time being, or by the Governor or Deputy-Governor of the said Corporation *for the preceding year;* and they hereby respectively authorized and directed, to administer and receive the said *Oaths and Declaration*

The Declaration to be taken and subscribed, and the Oaths of Directors.

respectively, to and from any Deputy-Governor accordingly. PROVIDED ALSO, and our Will and Pleasure is, and we do by these presents, for us, our Heirs and Successors, ordain and appoint that none of the said *Alexander Jaffray, Travers Hartley*, Sir *Nicolas Lawless*, Baronet, *Amos Strettell, Jeremiah Vickers, John Latouche, Abraham Wilkinson, George Godfrey Hoffman, William Colvill, Peter Latouche, Samuel Dick, Jeremiah D'Olier, Alexander Armstrong, George Palmer* and *John Allen*, hereby nominated, constituted and appointed to be the first Directors of the said Corporation, or any person or persons hereafter to be chosen to the office or trust of a Director of said Corporation; shall be capable to execute or act in the said Office of a Director at any time or times hereafter,

The Declaration.

until he or they shall respectively, *have made and subscribed the Declaration pursuant to the said Act, intitled, An Act to prevent the further growth of*

Oaths of Allegiance, Supremacy, and Abjuration.

Popery; and shall also have taken the Oaths of *Allegiance and Supremacy, and Abjuration;* or shall be capable to execute or act in the said Office or Trust of a Director, at any time or times hereafter, until he or they respectively shall have taken the Oath following, to wit, "*I, A. B. do swear that the sum of*

Oath for Stock.

Two Thousand Pounds sterling *of the* capital Stock *of the Body Politic, called by the Name of* The Governor and Company of the Bank of Ireland, *whereof I am appointed or elected to be a Director, doth at this time belong to me in my own Right, and not in trust for any other Person or Persons whatsoever:*" And likewise another Oath, in the form or to the effect following, viz.: "*I, A. B.*

Oath to the Company.

do swear, that in the Office of a Director of the Corporation or Company of the Bank of Ireland, *I will be indifferent and equal to all manner of Persons, and I will give my best advice and assistance for the support and good government of the said Corporation; and in the execution of the said Office of Director, I will faithfully and honestly demean myself, according to the best of my skill and understanding.*—So help me God." Which Oaths and Declarations to and from the Directors herein nominated, and every of them respectively, shall and may be administered and received by the said Chancellor of *Ireland*, or the said Keeper or Commissioners of our Great Seal of *Ireland*, or by the Chancellor, or Chief Baron of our Court of Exchequer of *Ireland*, or by the first Governor or Deputy-Governor herein before named, so as such first Governor or Deputy-Governor (in case they or either of them do administer the said Oaths, and receive the said Declaration) be first sworn, as is before mentioned; and the said Oaths and Declarations, to and from any future Director or Directors, shall and may be administered by the Chancellor of *Ireland*, or Keeper or Commissioners of the Great Seal of *Ireland*, or by the Chancellor, or Chief Baron of our Court of Exchequer in *Ireland*, for the time being, or any of them, or by a sworn Governor or Deputy-Governor of the said Corporation, for the time being, or by the Governor or Deputy-Governor, for the preceding year; and they are hereby authorized and required to administer the said Oaths, and receive the said Declaration, to and from all and every such Director and Directors, from time to time accordingly. PROVIDED ALSO, and our Will and Pleasure is, and we do by these presents, for us, our Heirs and Successors, ordain and appoint, that all and every the other members of the said Corporation, having each Five Hundred Pounds sterling, or more, Interest or Share in the Capital Stock of the said Corporation, before he or they severally shall be capable to give any vote in any general Court to be held for the said Corporation, shall make and subscribe the Declaration pursuant to the said Act, intitled, "An *Act* to prevent the further growth of *Popery;*" and shall also take the Oaths of Allegiance, Supremacy and Abjuration, before the said Governor or Deputy-Governor of the said Corporation for the time being, who are hereby respectively authorised to administer and receive the same respectively and also the Oath in the Words or to the effect following, that is to say, "*I, A. B. do swear, that I will be faithful to the* Governor and Company of the Bank of Ireland, *whereof I am a member, and in all General Courts, when and so often as I shall be present, will, according to the best of my skill and understanding, give my advice, counsel and assistance, for the support and good Government of the said Corporation.*—So help me God." PROVIDED NEVERTHELESS, that any person or persons, commonly called or known to be Quakers, having each Five Hundred Pounds sterling or more, Interest or Share, in the Capital Stock of the said Corporation, before they shall be capable of voting in any such General Court as aforesaid, shall and may, instead of the Oaths and Declarations hereby prescribed to be made and taken by the respective Members, having each Five Hundred Pounds sterling or more, as aforesaid, before the said Governor or Deputy-Governor, solemnly promise and declare in the Words, or to the same effect, (*mutatis mutandis,*) and shall severally subscribe the same, together with a solemn Declaration that they will be faithful, and true Allegiance bear to us, our Heirs and Successors. and that no foreign Prince, Prelate, State or Potentate, hath or ought to have any power, jurisdiction, superiority, authority, ecclesiastical or spiritual, within our Dominions.

Proviso for Persons professing the Popish Religion.

PROVIDED ALSO, NEVERTHELESS, that any person or persons professing the Popish Religion, shall, instead of the said Declaration, and Oaths of Allegiance, Supremacy and Abjuration, be at liberty in order to intitle them to vote as aforesaid, to take the Oath appointed to be taken, instead of the said Oaths, by an Act of Parliament passed in this Kingdom, in the thirteenth and fourteenth year of our Reign, intitled, "An Act to enable his Majesty's subjects, of whatever persuasion, to testify their Allegiance to him;" which said Oaths, Declaration, and Declarations, are to be administered by, and made before the several persons authorised to administer the several Oaths, in the stead whereof, the same are respectively substituted as aforesaid.

Power to administer oaths to Officers.

AND FURTHERMORE, OUR WILL AND PLEASURE IS, and we do by these presents, for us, our Heirs and Successors, ordain and appoint, that the said Court of Directors, shall have power and authority to administer an Oath to all inferior Agents or Servants, or Affirmation to any of them being Quakers, that shall be employed in the service of the said Corporation, for the faithful and due execution of their several Places, and Trusts in them reposed, in the words or to the effect following, that is to say,

Oath to Officers.

"*I, A. B. being elected in the office, or place of Treasurer, to the* Governor and Company of the Bank of Ireland, *do swear, or solemnly declare,* [as the case may be] *that I will be true and faithful to the said* Governor and Company; *and will faithfully and truly execute and discharge the said office, or place of Treasurer, to the utmost of my skill and power;*" and the like Oath, or Declaration, to the other Agents and Servants. (*mutatis mutandis.*)

Neglect or refusal of Oaths.

AND in case any person hereby nominated, or hereafter to be elected Governor, Deputy-Governor, or Director, as aforesaid, shall, for the space of ten days after such nomination or election, neglect, or refuse to take, or make the respective Oaths and Declarations, hereby appointed to be taken and received, as aforesaid; or shall refuse or neglect to take upon him, his, or their offices, that then, and in every such case, the Office and Place of every such person so neglecting or refusing, shall become vacant, and others be chosen in their places, by a General Court of the said Corporation.

Dividends how made.

AND FURTHER, our Will and Pleasure is, and we do hereby appoint, that no Dividend shall at any time be made by the said Governor and Company, save only out of the Interest, Profit, or Produce, arising by, or out of the said Capital Stock or Fund; or by such dealing, buying, or selling, as is allowed by the said Act of Parliament, made in the twenty-first and twenty-second years of our Reign, until redemption by Parliament of the said yearly Fund of Twenty-four Thousand Pounds sterling; and that no Dividend whatsoever, shall at any time be made without the consent of the Members of the said Corporation, in a General Court, qualified to vote as aforesaid.

Four General Courts every year.

AND OUR WILL AND PLEASURE IS, and we do hereby appoint, that the said Governor, or, in his absence, the Deputy-Governor for the time being, shall, from time to time, and they are hereby required, upon such notice to be given, as aforesaid, to summon and appoint four General Courts at least, in every year; whereof one to be in the month of *September*, another in the month of *December*, another in the month of *April*, and another in the month of *July*. AND OUR FURTHER WILL AND PLEASURE IS, and we do appoint, that if, at any time or times, there shall be a failure of holding a General Court in any of the said Months, by the default of the Governor, and Deputy-Governor, or either of them, that then, and so often, and in every such case, any three or more of the Directors of the said Corporation, shall, and may summon, and call a General Court, which shall meet and be holden in the Month next coming, after the Month in which the same should have been holden, upon the summons of the Governor, or Deputy-Governor, as aforesaid. AND MOREOVER, our Will and Pleasure is, and we do by these presents, direct and appoint, that the said Governor, or in his absence, the Deputy-Governor, for the time being, shall, from time to time, upon demand, to be made by any nine or more of the said Members, having each of them Five Hundred Pounds sterling, or more Interest, or Share, in the said Capital Stock, within ten days after such demand, summon and call such General Courts, to be held of the said Members of the Corporation, qualified for Electors, as aforesaid; and in default of the Governor, or Deputy-Governor, to summon and call such Court, it shall and may be lawful to and for the said nine, or more Members, having each Five Hundred Pounds sterling, Stock as aforesaid, upon ten days notice, in writing, to be fixed upon the Royal-Exchange in Dublin, to summon and hold a General Court; and there to do and dispatch any business relating to the Government, or Affairs of the said Corporation, and to hear and debate any complaint that shall be made against any Governor, Deputy-Governor, or Directors, for the mismanagement of his, or their respective Offices. AND if such Governor, Deputy-Governor, or Directors, shall not clear him, or themselves, of such complaint, to the satisfaction of the major part of the Members of the said Corporation, in the said General Court assembled; that then, within ten days, another General Court shall be called, and held as aforesaid, of the Members of the said Corporation, qualified to vote, as aforesaid, finally to determine the same by the majority of their Votes, as aforesaid, who may remove or displace all, or any of the said Governor, Deputy-Governor, and Directors, for such misdemeanors, or abuse of their offices, and elect and choose others in his, or their room, in the same manner as the said Elections, between the 25th day of *March*, and 25th day of *April*, are herein before directed to be made. AND in every case, where any Governor, Deputy-Governor, or Directors, shall happen to die, or be removed, or his office shall otherwise become void before the expiration of the time for which he shall have been elected, the major part of the Members of the said Corporation to be assembled in a General Court, and being qualified, as aforesaid, shall, and may elect and choose any other Member or Members of the said Corporation, qualified as aforesaid, into the office of such Governor, Deputy-Governor, or Director, that shall so die, or be removed, or whose office shall become void; which person so to be chosen, shall continue in the said office until the next usual time hereby appointed for Election, and until others shall be duly chosen

How the Governor, Deputy-Governor, and Directors shall act, and the power given to them.

and sworn. AND for the better ordering and managing the Affairs of the said Corporation, we do by these presents, for us, our Heirs and Successors, grant unto the said *Governor and Company of the Bank of Ireland*, and their Successors, AND OUR WILL AND PLEASURE IS, and we do by these presents, authorise and appoint, that the said Governor, Deputy-Governor, and Directors, for the time being, or any eight, or more of them, of which the Governor, or Deputy-Governor, to be always one, except as herein after mentioned, shall, and may, from time to time, and at all convenient times, assemble, and meet together at any convenient place or places, for the direction or management of the Affairs and Business of the said Corporation, and then, and there, hold Courts of Directors, for the purposes aforesaid, and summon General Courts to meet as often as they shall see cause; and that the said Governor, Deputy-Governor, and Directors, or the major part of them so assembled, whereof the Governor, or Deputy-Governor, is to be always one, except as herein after is mentioned, shall, and may act, according to such Bye-Laws, Constitutions, Orders, Rules, or Directions, as shall, from time to time, be made and given unto them, by the General Court of the said Corporation; and in all cases where such Bye-Laws, Constitutions, Orders, Rules, or Directions, by, or from the General Court shall be wanting, the said Governor, or Deputy-Governor, and Directors, or the major part of them, so assembled, (whereof the Governor, or Deputy-Governor, is to be always one, save as herein after is mentioned.) shall, and may direct and manage all the Affairs and Business of the said Corporation, in the borrowing or receiving of Monies, and giving securities for the same, under the common Seal of the said Corporation; and in their dealings in Bills of Exchange; or the buying and selling of Bullion, Gold, or Silver; or in selling any Goods, Wares, or Merchandizes whatsoever, which shall really, and *bona fide*, be left, or deposited, with the said Corporation, for Money lent or advanced thereon, and which shall not be redeemed at the time agreed, or within three Months after; or in selling such Goods as shall, or may be the produce of Lands purchased by the said Corporation; or in the lending or advancing any of the Monies of the said Corporation, and taking Pawns, or other Securities for the same; and to choose and appoint the Agents or Servants, which shall from time to time, be necessary to be employed in the Affairs and Business of the said Corporation; and to allow and pay reasonable salaries and allowances to the said Agents and Servants respectively, and them or any of them, from time to time, to remove or displace as they shall see cause, and generally to act and do in all matters and things whatsoever, which, by the said recited Act of Parliament, shall or may be done, in all matters and things whatsoever, which they shall judge necessary for the well ordering and managing of the said Corporation, and the affairs thereof; and to do, enjoy, perform, and execute, all the powers, authorities, privileges, acts and things, in relation to the said Corporation, as fully to all intents and purposes, as if the same were done by the *Governor and Company of the said Bank of Ireland*, or by a General Court of the same; subject nevertheless, to such restraint, limitations, rules or appointments as are contained in the said recited Act of Parliament, for or concerning the Trade, Business or Affairs of the said Corporation, or otherwise relating thereunto. PROVIDED NEVERTHELESS, and our Will and Pleasure is, and we do further direct, that when any General Court, or Court of Directors of the said Corporation, shall be assembled according to due Summons or Appointment in case the said Governor, and Deputy-Governor shall be absent from such meeting, one Hour after the usual time of proceeding to Business, that then and in every such case it shall be lawful for the said General Court, and Court of Directors respectively, to choose a Chairman for that time only, and to proceed to Business, and to transact the affairs of the said Corporation, and that the transactions of the said General Court, and Court of Directors respectively, shall be as valid and effectual, to all intents and purposes, as if the said Governor or Deputy-Governor had been present; and so as that in every such Court of Directors, there be nine Directors present. AND OUR WILL IS, that every Chairman so to be chosen, shall have the like privileges and authority in all respects, as are by these presents given to the Governor or Deputy-Governor when present. OUR WILL AND PLEASURE IS, and we do hereby, for us, our Heirs and Successors, give full power to all, and every the said Members, qualified for Electors as aforesaid, in their General Courts or assemblies aforesaid, by majority of their votes, as aforesaid, to make and constitute such Bye-Laws and Ordinances, for, and relating to the affairs and government of the said Corporation, and the imposing mulcts and amerciaments upon offenders against the same, as to them shall seem meet; so as that such Bye-Laws be not repugnant to the Laws of our Kingdom of *Ireland*, and be confirmed and approved according to the Statutes in such case made and provided. ALL which mulcts and amerciaments, shall and may be received and recovered to the only use and behoof of the said *Governor and Company of the Bank of Ireland*, and their Successors, without any account or other matter or thing to be thereof rendered to us, our Heirs and Successors. AND also to allow such salaries or allowances to the said Governor, Deputy-Governor, and Directors, as to them shall seem meet. AND OUR WILL AND PLEASURE IS, and we do hereby, for us, our Heirs and Successors, ordain and appoint, that the first General Court for the said Corporation, shall be held within the space of Twenty-eight Days, next after the passing of our said Letters Patent. PROVIDED ALWAYS, and our Will and Pleasure is, that for the ascertaining and limiting how, and in what manner, and under what rules the said Capital Stock, and yearly Fund of Twenty-four Thousand Pounds sterling, shall and may be assignable and assigned, transferable and transferred by such person and persons, as shall from time to time have any Interest or Share in the same; WE do hereby direct and appoint, that there shall be constantly kept in the Public Office of the said *Governor and Company of the Bank of Ireland*, a Register, or Book or Books, wherein all Assignments and Transfers shall be entered. AND OUR WILL AND PLEASURE IS, and we do hereby for us, our Heirs and Successors, pursuant and according to the Power given unto us by the said

Act of Parliament, order, limit, direct and appoint, that the method and manner of making all Assignments and Transfers of the said Capital Stock, and yearly Fund, or any part thereof, shall be by an entry in the said Book or Books, signed by the Party so assigning or transferring, in the Words and to

Form of Transfer.

the effect following, viz., MEMORANDUM, that "*I, A. B. this Day of in the Year of our Lord do assign and transfer of my Interest or Share in the Capital Stock or Fund of the* Governor and Company of the Bank of Ireland, *and all Benefits arising thereby, unto his or her Executors, Administrators and Assigns. Witness my Hand* ." Or in case the Person assigning be not personally present, then by an entry in the said Book or Books, signed by some Person thereunto lawfully authorized, by *Letter of Attorney*, or Writing under Hand and Seal, attested by two or more Witnesses,

Form of Transfer by Letter of Attorney.

in the Words, or to the effect following, *viz.*, MEMORANDUM, that "*I, A. B. this Day of in the Year of our Lord by virtue of a Letter of Attorney, or authority under the Hand and Seal of dated the Day of in the said Year of our Lord do in the Name and on the behalf of the said assign and transfer of the Interest or Share of the said in the Capital Stock and Fund of the* Governor and Company of the Bank of Ireland, *and all Benefit arising thereby, unto his, her or their Executors, Administrators and Assigns. Witness my Hand* ." Under which Transfer the Person or Persons, Bodies Politic or Corporate, to whom such Assignment or Transfer shall be made, or some other Person by him, her, or them lawfully authorized thereunto, shall sign his, her, or their Name or Names, attesting that he, she,

Acceptance.

or they, do freely and voluntarily *accept* of the same, and that the entry signed as aforesaid, and no other way or method, shall be the manner and method used, in the passing, assigning or transferring, the Interest or Share in the said Capital Stock or Fund; and such Transfer, or Assignment, shall be good and available, and convey the whole Estate and Interest of the Party transferring, or ordering the same to be transferred. PROVIDED ALWAYS, that

Deviseable by Will.

any person having any Share or Interest in the said Capital Stock, or Fund, may dispose of, or devise the same, by his, or her, last Will and Testament; but, however, that such Devisee shall not transfer the same, or be intitled to

Entry of the Devise in the Company's Books.

receive any dividend, until an entry, or memorandum of so much of the said Will, as relates to the Said Stock or Fund, be made in the book or books, or some other book or books, to be kept by the said Governor and Company, for that purpose. AND OUR WILL AND PLEASURE FURTHER IS, and we do appoint,

Governor, Deputy or Chairman, not to vote in General Courts, or Court of

that the said Governor, or in his absence, the Deputy-Governor, or Chairman, shall not have any vote in a General Court, or Court of Directors, save where there shall happen to be an equal number of Votes. PROVIDED NEVERTHELESS, that all matters and things, which the said Governor, Deputy-Governor, or Directors shall, in manner, as aforesaid, order, and direct, to be done by Sub-

Committees, or other persons appointed under them, shall, and may (by virtue of such orders) be done by the said Sub-Committees, or other persons so appointed. AND OUR WILL IS, and we do for us, our Heirs, and Successors, grant, and declare, that our said Letters Patent, or the Enrolment thereof, shall be in, and by all things, valid and effectual in the Law, according to the true intent and meaning of the same; and shall be taken, construed, and adjudged, in the most favourable and beneficial sense, for the best advantage of the said Corporation, as well in our Courts of Record, as elsewhere, notwithstanding any non-recital, mis-recital, defect, uncertainty, or imperfection, in our said Letters Patent. AND OUR WILL AND PLEASURE IS, and we do hereby direct, that our said Letters Patent to the Governor, and Company, aforesaid, under the Great Seal of *Ireland*, shall be in due manner made and sealed, without Fine or Fee, great or small to us, in our *Hanaper*, or elsewhere, to our use therefore, any ways to be rendered, paid, or made. AND OUR WILL AND PLEASURE FURTHER IS, and we do hereby for us, our Heirs and Successors, covenant, grant, and agree, to and with the said Governor and Company, and their Successors, that we, our Heirs and Successors, shall and will, from time to time, and at all times hereafter, upon the humble suit and request of the said Governor, and Company, and their Successors, give, and grant, unto them, all such further and other powers, privileges, authorities, matters and things, which we, or they can, or may lawfully grant, and as shall be reasonably advised and devised, by the Council learned in the law of the said Governor, and Company, for the time being; and shall be approved by our Attorney, or Solicitor General, of our said Kingdom of *Ireland*, in our behalf. PROVIDED ALWAYS, that these, our Letters Patent, be enrolled in the Rolls of our High Court of Chancery, in our said Kingdom of *Ireland*, within the space of six Months next ensuing the date of these presents. IN WITNESS whereof, we have caused these, our Letters, to be made Patent. WITNESS, our aforesaid Lieutenant-General and General-Governor of our said Kingdom of *Ireland*, at *Dublin*, the tenth day of *May*, in the twenty-third year of our Reign.

CONWAY.

Enrolled in the Office of the Rolls of his Majesty's High Court of Chancery of Ireland, *the fifteenth day of* May, *in the twenty-third year of the Reign of* King George *the Third, &c.*

FINIS.

A List of the Original Governors, Directors, and Subscribers to the
BANK OF IRELAND:

With their several SUBSCRIPTION SUMS affixed, in the Order they subscribed.

Thus marked † are the Commissioners appointed for receiving Subscriptions.

GOVERNOR,
David Latouche, Junior, Esq.;

DEPUTY GOVERNOR,
Theophilus Thompson, Esq.;

DIRECTORS,

Alexander Jaffray, Esq.
Travers Hartley, Esq.
Sir Nicholas Lawless, Bart.
Amos Strettell, Esq.
Jeremiah Vickers, Esq.
John Latouche, Esq.
Abraham Wilkinson, Esq.
George Godfrey Hoffman, Esq.
William Colvill, Esq.
Peter Latouche, Esq.
Samuel Dick, Esq.
Jeremiah D'Olier, Esq.
Alexander Armstrong, Esq.
George Palmer, Esq.
John Allen, Esq.

SUBSCRIBERS,

	£		£
†David Latouche, Esq.	10,000	Right Hon. Lord Farnham	2,000
†David Latouche, jun., Esq.	10,000	†Samuel Dick, Esq.	6,000
†John Latouche, Esq.	10,000	John Gasper Battier, Esq.	4,000
†Peter Latouche, Esq.	10,000	Donald Grant, Esq.	1,200
Right Hon. William Brownlow	9,000	Sir Francis Hutchinson, Bart.	1,000
†Right Hon. Joshua Cooper	10,000	Mrs. Ann Hutchinson	1,000
†Reverend Dean Ryder	10,000	Archdeacon Edward Synge	1,000
Reverend Henry Maxwell	1,600	Alexander Mangin, Esq.	2,000
Fredk. Trench, of Heywood, Esq.	2,000	Archdeacon James Hutchinson	1,000
Mr. Gordon McNeil	1,200	Henry Brownrigg, Esq.	2,000
Lady Dowager Longford	800	Mr. William Williams	1,000
Honourable Miss Packenham	600	Ditto, for an Annuity Company	2,000
Reverend Doctor Henry Dabzac	2,000	Robert Ashworth, Esq.	5,000
William Keon, Esq.	400	John Tydd, Esq.	1,600
Mr. John Marsden	1,000	†Theophilus Thompson, Esq.	5,000
Thomas St. George, Esq.	5,000	†Travers Hartley, Esq.	2,000
†Sir John Browne, Bart.	10,000	Mr. William Hunt	2,000

	£		£
Mr. Joseph Hone, jun.	2,000	Major Edward Cane	1,200
Charles Ward, Esq.	2,000	Charles Hamilton, Esq.	2,000
Warden Flood, Esq.	2,000	Michael Sweetman, Esq.	3,000
†William Colvill, Esq.	5,200	Francis Gorman, Esq.	1,200
†William Smyth, Esq.	5,000	David Dick, Esq.	3,000
Colonel Martin Tucker	2,000	Joseph Phelps, Esq.	1,000
Lady Dowager Courtown	1,600	Mr. Jacob Handcock	600
John Folie, Esq.	2,000	Colonel David Dundas	1,200
†George Godfrey Hoffman, Esq.	3,100	John Comerford, Esq.	2,000
†John White, Esq.	3,100	Dennis Thomas O'Brien, Esq.	3,200
William Wallace, Esq.	4,400	John Fitzsimons, Esq.	2,000
John Allen, Esq.	4,000	†Robert Shaw, Esq.	5,000
Mr. Leland Crosthwaite	1,000	James Lane, Esq.	1,000
Mr. John Rivers	3,200	†Abraham Wilkinson, Esq.	5,200
Mr. Archibald Bell	800	Mrs. Mary Morin	2,000
Robert Watson Wade, Esq.	4,000	James Dennis, Esq.	1,000
†Rt. Hon. William Conyngham	10,000	Mr. John Page	1,000
Major John Corneille	7,000	†Jeremiah Vickers, Esq.	10,000
Mr. Nathaniel Card	2,000	A. Wilkinson & J. Vickers	600
Mr. William McKay	1,000	Bartholomew Callan, Esq.	5,000
John Cumming, Esq.	3,200	†Rt. Hon. Hen. Theoph. Clements	10,000
Jeremiah D'Olier, Esq.	3,800	Major General Eyre Massey	2,000
George Palmer, Esq.	2,000	Charles Farran, Esq.	1,000
Richard Hare, Esq.	5,000	Mr. James Potts	2,000
†Alexander Jaffray, Esq.	4,000	Mr. John Westlake	2,000
Sir William Montgomery, Bart.	1,200	Mr. Arthur Stanley	2,000
†Sir Nicholas Lawless, Bart.	10,000	Mr. Thomas Walker	3,000
†Valentine Brown, Esq.	10,000	John Digby, Esq.	3,000
Right Hon. Earl of Miltown	1,000	Mr. Francis Cahill	2,000
Thomas Wolfe, Esq.	1,000	Mr. William Netterville	500
John Wolfe, Esq.	1,000	Mr. Stephen Devereux	800
†Theobald Wolfe, Esq.	10,000	Alderman John Darragh	2,000
†Charles Walker, Esq.	10,000	Samuel Newport, Esq.	2,500
Alexander Armstrong, Esq.	2,000	Mr. Henry Betagh	1,000
†Joseph Hines, Esq.	10,000	Doctor Henry Quin	5,000
†Cornelius O'Callaghan, Esq.	6,800	Lieutenant General Pomeroy	10,000
†Amos Strettell, Esq.	3,000	Alexander Crookshank, Esq.	1,000
†Anthony Dermott, Esq.	8,000	Charles Strong, Esq.	1,000
His Grace the Archbp. of Cashell	4,000	Widow Plunket and Sons	3,200
Sir Annesley Stewart, Bart.	2,400	Stephen Wybrants, Esq.	3,000
Mr. James Williams	4,650	Hugh Howard, Esq.	4,000
Mr. Thomas White	1,000	Valentine Connor, Esq.	2,000
Fredk. Trench, of Woodlawn, Esq.	1,000	Mrs. Letitia Page	200

	£		£
Mr. Benjamin Smith	1,000	Christopher Decy, Esq.	3,000
John Wetherall, Esq.	2,000	Thomas Acton, Esq.	2,000
Charles O'Neill, Esq.	1,200	Robert Howard, Esq.	400
John Wallis, Esq.	1,000	Mr. John Darby	600
Mr. Edward Atkinson	1,000	Right Hon. Luke Gardiner	5,000
Mr. Ephraim Hutchinson	1,200	William Sweetman, Esq.	3,200
Reverend Doctor Thomas Pack	1,000	Nicholas Gordon, Esq.	1,000
Mrs. Meliora Adlercron	600	Mr. Joseph Moroney	600
Mrs. Frances Lloyd	200	Doctor Róbert Emmett	2,000
Mrs. Eliza Lombard	200	William Norton Barry, Esq.	2,000
Christopher Sherlock, Esq.	2,000	Mrs. Katharine Hamilton	400
John Betagh, Esq.	1,200	Sir Matthew Blackiston, Bart.	1,200
Mr. Charles Ryan	1,200	Mrs. Katharine Ould	1,000
John Thomas Foster, Esq.	2,000	Dudley Hussey, Esq.	500
Robert Gordon, Esq.	2,400	Mr. Robert Lynch	400
Captain Joseph McVeagh	2,000	Mr. Francis French	400
Sydenham Singleton, Esq.	1,000	Mr. David M'Cance	2,000
Major John Glover	2,000	Theophilus Bolton, Esq.	1,600
James Forde, Esq.	600	John Moore, Esq.	1,200
Mrs. Rebecca Coghlan	200	Mr. Christopher French	400
Richard Le Hunte, Esq.	1,000	Reverend Doctor Bernard Ward	2,400
James Lawlor, Esq.	10,000	Miss Priscilla and Mabel Forbes	600
Jonathan Tanner, Esq.	3,000	Mr. Isaac Simmons	1,000
Miss Letitia Burke	100	Reverend Dr. Samuel Pulleine	2,200
Richard Morgan, Esq.	4,000	Henry Ellis, Esq.	7,000
Mr. Luke Gaven	600	William Molesworth, Esq.	1,200
Mr. John Johnston	2,000	Mr. William Keating	1,000
Mr. Ignatius Purcell	800	Rev. Joseph Stopford	800
Colonel Thomas Marlay	2,200	Mrs. Alicia Postlethwait	600
Hugh Henry, Esq.	5,000	William Digges Latouche, Esq.	2,000
Sir Fielding Ould	600	Mr. James Standish	400
Mrs. Ann Thomas	300	Mrs. Ann Dixon	1,200
John Lees, Esq.	5,000	Right Hon. Lord Lifford, Lord High Chancellor	6,000
Rev. Dr. Christopher Harvey	500		
Messrs. Pierceys and Waggots	4,000	Mr. James Ogilby	1,000
Mr. John Findlay	1,000	Right Hon. Lord Longford	1,000
Mr. Benjamin Clarke	1,000	Mr. William Harkness	1,000
Doctor Henry Rock	400	Joseph Goff, Esq.	2,000
Marine Society	4,000	Major William Hall	1,000
Mrs. Ann Dawson	400	Thomas Keightly, Esq.	5,000
William Ogilvie, Esq.	800	James Hamilton, Esq.	2,000
Reverend Dr. William Browne	1,200	John Thewles, Esq.	1,200
Captain Thomas Tickell	1,000	Reverend William Day	500

	£		£
Arthur Wolfe, Esq.	4,000	George Maquay, Esq.	2,000
Edward Dornan, Esq.	600	Charles Quin, Esq.	500
Captain John Shaw	1,000	Henry George Quin, Esq.	500
Michael Cosgrove, Esq.	2,000	Thomas Fitzgerald, Esq.	2,000
Mr. Robert French	500	Mrs. Theodosia Blachford	400
Mr. James Shee	200	Mr. Thady Grehan	3,750
Miss Rosa Whitwell	1,200	Andrew Caldwell, Esq.	1,000
Miss Martha Stronge	200	Mr. Rowland Norris	1,000
John Hall, Esq.	500	Miss Esther M. Vauteau	500
Mr. Caleb Jenkin	2,000	Peter Digges Latouche, Esq.	1,000
Mr. Luke White	2,000	Mr. William Skeys	3,000
Columb Morgan, Esq.	2,000	†John Dawson Coates, Esq.	5,000
			£600,000

RULES, ORDERS,

AND

BYE-LAWS,

FOR

The Good Government of the Corporation of the Governor and Company of the BANK OF IRELAND.

I. BYE-LAW.

Elections, the Time, Manner, and Scrutiny.

1st Paragr. *The Preamble.*

WHEREAS many uncertainties and inconveniencies may arise for want of a due and Regular method of proceeding at General Courts of Election, for remedy thereof,

2nd Paragr. *Votes to be delivered personally in writing or print.*

It is hereby ordained and appointed, that at every General Court for any Election, every member qualified to vote, and being present, shall deliver in writing or print, a note or list, containing the name or names of such person or persons (members of this Corporation respectively qualified, according to the tenor of the Charter) as he thinks fit to serve and execute the office or employment, for which such election is to be had or made, and that at every General Election for Governor and Deputy-Governor, or either of them, each elector shall deliver in writing or print, only the name of one person qualified for the place of Governor, and only the name of one person qualified for the place of Deputy-Governor, and no more; and that at every General Election for Directors, which shall always be held on the second day succeeding said election of Governor and Deputy-Governor, each elector shall likewise deliver in a list of the names of fifteen persons, which shall appear by the printed list hereafter ordered to be delivered out to be qualified for Directors, and no more or less.

If more or less names than the limited number, the vote to be rejected.

And that in case any person shall deliver in writing or print, any more than one name for the place of Governor; one name for the place of Deputy-Governor; or a list of any more or less than fifteen names of persons qualified for Directors, the same shall be reputed and deemed as no vote, and the said list, and all the names therein, shall be totally rejected; and that the like mode be observed upon all elections in case of vacancies.

And that in case at any General Court of election of Directors, any person shall in such list insert the names of any more than ten of those persons, who were chosen into, and did serve the office of Directors, the then last preceding year, the same list shall in like manner be rejected.

And that if in any list for Directors, there shall be inserted the name either of the Governor or Deputy-Governor elected for the ensuing year, such list shall be rejected. And that in case any Director shall upon any vacancy be chosen into the office of Governor, or Deputy-Governor, the seat of such person as Director shall be absolutely vacated, and another person chosen in his place.

And in case it shall happen, that upon making the scrutiny for any election of Governor, Deputy-Governor, or Directors, any two or more persons qualified for the respective office or employment, for which he or they shall be named, shall have an equal number of votes, which shall or may entitle one or more of them to such office or employment, the election, in such case, shall be determined and settled by the General Court, in which such scrutiny shall be reported.

And that if on taking the scrutiny for any election of Governor, Deputy-Governor, or Directors, it shall fall out that two or more persons qualified for the office, for which such election shall be made, shall have the same christian and sir-names, and are not distinguished by their additions, or that a wrong christian name in any note or list is placed to a sir-name, when but one person of that sir-name is qualified for the respective office, or that any literal mistake be made in christian or sir-names, in all and every the cases before mentioned, such undistinguished wrong or mistaken name or names, shall be kept, and not thrown aside or rejected, but the rest of the list shall be allowed: And the persons appointed to take the scrutiny at such election, or so many as shall be present, may determine the person, or persons intended by such undistinguished, wrong, or mistaken name or names, provided they, or the major part of them, shall agree in ascertaining the person or persons so meant or intended; but in default thereof, the same shall be determined and settled by the General Court. in which such scrutiny shall be reported.

And that every such election shall commence at the hour of ten o'clock in the morning, and continue open until two of the clock in the afternoon, when the glass or balloting box shall be sealed up, or the ballots immediately cast up by scrutineers, to be then appointed for that purpose, and that no note or list shall be received after said hour.

8th Paragr. *None to use or procure indirect means to obtain votes.*

And that if any member of this corporation shall hereafter use, or procure to be used, any indirect means to obtain any vote or votes for the election of himself, or any other, to be Governor, Deputy-Governor, or Directors of this corporation, and be thereof declared guilty at a General Court, to be called for that purpose, such person from thenceforth shall, for ever, be incapable of being elected, to, or holding any such office or place.

9th Paragr. *Elections of committees by a General Court to be in the same manner.*

And that in all elections of Committees, hereafter to be had or made by a General Court, the same orders, rules and methods (so near as the case will admit) shall be used, observed, and kept, and under such penalties and disabilities as herein before prescribed, for or concerning the election of Governor, Deputy-Governor, and Directors.

10th Paragr. *If more than two-thirds of the old Directors be chosen, all above that number to be removed.*

And in case, at any Annual General Court of election, all the fifteen Directors for the preceding year, or more than two-thirds of them shall happen to have the majority of votes, for being Directors for the ensuing year, that then the remaining one third or other less number of the said fifteen (over and above two-thirds of them) as shall happen to have the fewest votes, shall be removed, and such five or other less number of the other members of this Corporation, qualified as aforesaid, who have the most voices next to those so removed, shall be, and be deemed and reputed to be elected to succeed and serve as directors for the succeeding year, in the stead and place of those so removed, and shall be admitted and sworn accordingly.

11th Paragr. *Part of this Bye-Law to be printed in the list for the annual election.*

And that the first, second, third, fourth, seventh and eighth paragraphs, or clauses of this Bye-Law, shall be inserted at the end of every printed list of all persons qualified to be elected Governor, Deputy-Governor, or Director; which list shall be given out on demand, at the bank, at least three days before the annual elections of those officers, to the end the members of this corporation, qualified to vote, may be well-informed and directed in the giving in their votes.

II. Bye-Law.

Voting by the Ballot, or by Lists, and choosing Officers.

1st Paragr. *In all questions relating to one person or thing, the ballot (if demanded by 9) to be allowed.*

Item, It is resolved and ordained, that in all General Courts, upon any election or other question to be made or determined, concerning any one person, matter, or thing only, the ballot shall be allowed and used, in case the same be demanded by any nine or more members, then qualified to elect and vote, and not otherwise.

And that in all General Courts, upon any election or question to be made or determined, concerning more than one person, matter or thing, such election or question shall not be determined by the ballot, but by notes or lists in writing, of the members qualified to vote, put into a glass or box, in the same manner as the Court of Directors are to be chosen; in case the said determination by notes or lists shall be demanded by any nine or more persons qualified to vote.

And further, That from and after the five and twentieth day of *March*, 1784, and so yearly, and every year, for ever, all and every the officers, ministers, agents, or servants employed or to be employed by this corporation, or by the Governor, Deputy-Governor, and Directors, or any of them, in the service of this corporation, shall be elected by the Court of Directors every year, by the ballot, within thirty days after the General Court, for the annual election of Governor, Deputy-Governor, and Directors.

III. Bye-Law.

Custody of the Common Seal, and how to be used.

Item, It is ordained, that the seal of this corporation shall be carefully kept under three locks, the three keys whereof shall be severally kept by such three of the Governor, Deputy-Governor, and Directors, for the time being, as the Court of Directors, from time to time, shall empower to keep the same, and that the said seal shall not be affixed, or set to any paper or parchment, writing, or instrument whatsoever, but by an order of the Court of Directors for that purpose first had and obtained, and also in the presence of three or more of the Governor, Deputy-Governor, and Directors for the time being.

IV. Bye-Law.

Keeping the Cash.

Item, It is ordained, that the cash of this corporation (excepting such sum and sums of money as shall by the committee in waiting, subject to such regulations as the Court of Directors shall appoint, be thought necessary to be left in the hands of one or more of the Cashiers for running cash) shall be carefully kept under three or more locks, the keys whereof shall be kept by such three or more of the Governor, Deputy-Governor, and Directors, as the said Court of Directors, from time to time, shall empower to keep the same, each of the said persons keeping one of the said keys.

V. Bye-Law.

The Meeting and Business of Courts of Directors and their Sub-committees.

A Court of Directors to be held once a week at least.
No money to be lent but what, and how the Court of Directors shall order.
Every Sub-committee to lay their proceedings weekly before the Court of Directors.

Item, For the more easy and safe dispatch of the business of this corporation, to the honour and benefit thereof, it is resolved and ordained, that a Court of Directors shall be held once in every week at least, and that such court may and shall, from time to time, (as occasion shall require) appoint Sub-committees, and give all needful directions to such Sub-committees, concerning what securities shall be taken for money to be lent, and of what nature or kind ; and also in what proportions, and touching and concerning all and every other thing and things requisite in that behalf. And it is hereby ordained, that no money shall be lent upon any other sort of security, or in any other proportion, or to any other value, or otherwise disposed of, than what, or as shall be, from time to time, first directed by the said Court of Directors. And that every Sub-committee shall weekly lay before said Court of Directors, so to be held as aforesaid, an account of what monies are or shall be then owing by this corporation under their common seal, and what securities shall have been taken, or other business transacted or negotiated by them, touching this corporation, during the then last preceding week.

VI. Bye-Law.

Dealings of Governor, Deputy-Governor, and Directors, with the Corporation, not to be concealed.

The Governor, Deputy, and Directors, to publish to the Sub-committee their dealings with the corporation, and all circumstances thereof.

Item, For the prevention of fraud and deceit in all and every the transactions of this corporation, it is resolved and ordained, that in all cases whatsoever, where the Governor, Deputy-Governor, and Directors of the corporation, or any of them, shall have any dealing or business with this corporation, upon their own account, separately, or in conjunction with any others, for or in respect of any tallies, bills of exchange, pawns, pledges or other contract or bargain whatsoever, by, or from, to, or with this corporation, that then and in every such case, such Governor, Deputy-Governor, and Director, (so having any such business with this corporation in manner as aforesaid) shall at the time of his or their negotiating or transacting the same, declare and publish to the Sub-committee for the time being, fully, fairly and clearly, such his share and interest, whether sole or joint with others, in all and every such affair or business by him or them so negotiated or transacted as aforesaid, and all the particular circumstances thereof. And if any such Governor, Deputy-Governor, or Director, shall at any time wittingly or willingly offend contrary to this rule, ordinance or bye-law, such person so offending, being first accused thereof in any general Court, and summoned to answer the same, and afterwards declared guilty thereof by another general Court, shall immediately become, and be deemed and reputed to be, incapable for ever, either of holding or enjoying, or being chosen again into the said offices of Governor, Deputy-Governor, Directors, or any of them.

VII. Bye-Law.

The Concerned in Debates to withdraw.

Item, It is resolved and ordained, that in all cases where any question or debate shall at any time arise, or be made, touching or concerning any person or persons (members of this corporation) or concerning any matter or thing relating to any such person or persons, or wherein he or they shall be concerned, such person or persons, touching or concerning whom such question or debate is, or shall be had or made, shall have or give no vote relating thereto, but shall withdraw and be absent during such debate concerning himself, or any matter or thing wherein he is concerned.

VIII. Bye-Law.

Borrowing on the Seal.

Item, It is hereby ordained, that the Governor, Deputy-Governor, and Directors, or any of them, shall not at any time hereafter, without the consent and direction of a general Court first had, wittingly or willingly borrow, owe, or give security under the common seal, for any sum or sums of money, exceeding in the whole, at any one time Six Hundred Thousand Pounds, or procure the borrowing, owing or giving security for any such further sum or sums of money, by bill, bond, or other covenant or agreement, under the common seal of this corporation, as aforesaid; and in case the common seal shall be set or affixed to any bill, bond, or other agreement for money, contrary to this ordinance, or bye-law, that then each and every the Governor, Deputy-Governor, and Directors, or other members of this corporation, who shall order, procure, consent, agree to, or wittingly approve of the same, and be thereof lawfully convicted, shall for every such offence severally forfeit to the said Governor and Company of the Bank of *Ireland* the sum of One Thousand Pounds, sterling, and also all such further and other sum or sums of money as the said Governor and Company of the Bank of *Ireland* shall be damnified, for, or by reason thereof.

IX. Bye-Law.

Selling PAWNS.

Item, It is resolved and ordained, that all jewels, plate, bullion, or other goods, chattels, or merchandizes whatsoever, which shall be pawned unto this corporation, or left and deposited therewith, as pawns or pledges for money to be lent or advanced thereon, and not redeemed at the time agreed on, or within three calendar months afterwards, shall, whensoever they are sold, be sold at a public sale, upon three days' notice thereof, first given by writing, on the *Royal Exchange*, or upon such other public notice as the Court of Directors shall think fit. And that no sale of any such goods, chattels, or merchandizes, not redeemed as aforesaid, shall be had or made in any other manner.

X. Bye-Law.

For Transfers, and registering Contracts what to be paid.

Item, It is ordained, that upon all transfers to be made of any share or interest in the capital stock or fund of this corporation, the sum of five British shillings, and no more, shall be paid by the party transferring to, and for the use of the corporation, for, and towards the bearing and defraying the charges of books, accomptants, law, duty, and other like expenses. And that upon every promise contract, bargain, covenant or agreement to be made for the buying or selling of any share or interest, in the capital stock or fund of this corporation, or for transferring the property thereof in trust, or otherwise, which shall be brought to be registered in the book or books of the bank, the sum of two British Shillings, and no more shall be paid for such registering, (by the party desiring to register the same) to and for the use of this corporation.

XI. Bye-Law.

Against the Servants taking any Rewards.

Item, It is ordained, that no officer, servant, or other person whatsoever employed, or which shall hereafter be employed by this corporation, for or about any business of the same, shall presume directly or indirectly to receive or take any fee, gratuity, or reward of any sort, kind, or quality whatsoever, for the doing or dispatching, or the not doing or delaying, any business or affair belonging to this corporation, or for any other reason or colour, or upon any account relating to his or their respective employment, or otherwise concerning this corporation howsoever, from any person or persons whatsoever, other than only from this corporation, or by order thereof, or of the Court of Directors. And that if any person or persons employed or to be employed as aforesaid, shall offend contrary to this ordinance or bye-law, such person shall be for ever incapable of holding, or being chosen again into such his, their, or any other employment, in or under this corporation,

XII. Bye-Law.

General Court for Dividends, Half-yearly.

Item, It is ordained, that twice in every year a General Court shall be called and held, for considering the general state and condition of this corporation, and for the making of dividends, out of all and singular the produce and profit of the capital Stock and fund of this corporation, and the trade thereof, amongst the several owners and proprietors therein, according to their several shares and proportions: The one of which said courts shall be held on some day between the Tenth and Twenty-fifth of *December*, and the other on some day between the Tenth and Twenty-fourth day of *June*, yearly.

XIII. Bye-Law.

Yearly Recompences to the Governor, Deputy-Governor, and Directors.

Item, It is ordained, that the Recompence to the Governor and Deputy-Governor should be £500, Irish currency, each yearly, and to each Director £300, Irish currency, yearly.

XIV. Bye-Law.

Taking and reading the Minutes of Courts.

Item, It is ordained. that the minutes of all debates, orders, resolutions and transactions, had, made, and agreed on, at every General Court and Court of Directors, shall hereafter be taken and written down by the secretary, or the person chosen and sworn to be his assistant, in a book to be kept for that purpose; and that before any such courts shall be adjourned or dismissed, the minutes of that court shall be read over audibly by the secretary, or such his assistant as aforesaid.

And that all meetings of General Courts, of which notice is required, to be posted on the *Royal Exchange*, shall also be published in one or more of the Dublin News-papers.

XVI. Bye-Law.

Increases recompence to the Governors and Directors.

XVI. Bye-Law.

Alters times of Meeting of General Courts from December to January, and from June to July.

www.ingramcontent.com/pod-product-compliance
Lightning Source LLC
Chambersburg PA
CBHW030844270326
41928CB00007B/1207

* 9 7 8 3 3 3 7 3 2 2 8 1 6 *